Store Design and Visual Merchandising

Store Design and Visual Merchandising

Creating Store Space That Encourages Buying

Claus Ebster and Marion Garaus

First published in 2011 by
Business Expert Press, LLC
222 East 46th Street, New York, NY 10017
www.businessexpertpress.com

ISBN-13: 978-1-60649-094-5 (paperback)

ISBN-13: 978-1-60649-095-2 (e-book)

DOI 10.4128 9781606490952

A publication in the Business Expert Press Consumer Behavior collection

Collection ISSN: Forthcoming (print)
Collection ISSN: Forthcoming (electronic)

Cover design by Jonathan Pennell
Interior design by Scribe Inc.

First edition: June 2011

10 9 8 7 6 5 4 3 2 1

Printed in the United States of America.

Abstract

In an age of self-service stores, saturated markets, and ever more demanding customers, the careful and science-driven design of the point of sale has become a crucial success factor for both retailers and service businesses. In this book, the interested reader will find a variety of hands-on suggestions for how to optimize the design of retail stores and service environments to increase customer satisfaction and sales. While the focus is on the practical applicability of the concepts discussed, the book is nevertheless firmly grounded in consumer and psychological research. In this respect it is uniquely positioned vis-á-vis books written by artists, architects, and interior designers, which often lack a solid research foundation, and academic journals articles, which are often inaccessible to the educated yet nonspecialized reader. In writing this book, the authors draw on both the recent research literature and their own experience in marketing consulting and consumer research.

Topics covered in the book include goals and relevance of store design; design tips derived from environmental psychology; cognitive and affective approaches to store design and visual merchandising; use of ambient factors such as music, colors, and scents; and creation of emotional experiences and theming.

Keywords

store design, visual merchandising, consumer behavior, retailing, marketing

Contents

Acknowledgments

This book could not have been written without the help of our colleagues, friends, and family members.

Special thanks to Riem Khalil and Udo Wagner, who read the entire manuscript and offered numerous valuable suggestions. Riem also spent endless hours creating the wonderful illustrations that make this book so much more readable.

We also very much appreciate the many excellent suggestions by Linda Boyer, Christl Chloupek, Christian Garaus, Yvonne Havel, and Elisabeth Wolfsteiner.

Others who have enriched this book with contributions large and small are Stephen Chappell, Wolfgang Depauli, Jutatip Jamsawang, Wolfgang Weitzl, and Magdalena Zimprich.

We are also grateful to Linda, WriteWatchman, for the superior editorial support and to Umdasch Shop Concept for providing us with such excellent pictures.

Claus gratefully dedicates this book to his mother and to his wife, Riem; Marion dedicates this book to her husband, Christian.

Introduction

What Store Design Can Do for You

Several years ago an article appeared in *The Wall Street Journal* under the following headline: "Interior Designer Sets Out to Make Casino That Relaxes Your Morality."

A casino that "relaxes people's morality": How could that be? Perhaps the waitresses' serving drinks to the gamblers helps relax their morality, or maybe the dealers do that. But as the article explained, it was the casino buildings themselves that influenced customer behavior. A marketing specialist hired by one of the casinos explained that the entire building was designed for that express purpose (see Figure I.1):

Lobby windows, for instance, will be replaced by sheets of creamy Italian marble so that "people won't be able to relate to time. Once they step inside, they will be in an adult Disneyland." He'll use materials that "enhance" noise for the casino because "noise creates excitement." Lighting for the blackjack tables will extend far enough to envelope the player, but not far enough to include spectators, "who may interrupt his sense of security." The eight

Figure I.1. Influencing gamblers' consumer behavior in a casino.

restaurants will be done in "vestment colors"—gold, plum, deep reds—to suggest a kinship between gambling and royalty. Restaurants will have thick rugs and mohair wall coverings, meant to impart a "sensuality" and warmth so patrons will have "another brandy," he says. But the high rollers who get complimentary suites will taste the flip side of environmental psychology . . . Their suites will be done in bold, contrasting colors with lighting so bright and noise enhanced to such high levels that the occupants will practically run to the roulette wheels.[1]

In the years since that article, marketers have learned a great deal about consumer behavior and how the shopping environment influences that behavior in the casino, the restaurant, the supermarket, or the shopping mall. In this book we share with you some of the secrets we have learned as marketing consultants and consumer researchers on how you can design your store to increase sales *and* create delighted shoppers at the same time.

We won't relax your morality—or that that of your customers. (We happily leave such shenanigans to the casino people.) However, if you are a retailer, you will happily pick up a few tricks of the trade and research that will be new to you. If you are a shopper, we promise you won't ever look at a store the same way again.

But first, let's look at why store design and visual merchandising are so relevant and what their goals are.

Research studies have shown again and again that shoppers make up to 80% of their purchase decisions right in the store. The reasons are many. Some consumers have only a vague idea of what they want to buy before entering a store. Others have decided on a particular product beforehand, but they aren't sure about the specific brand or style. Yet others, the impulse buyers, decide on the spur of the moment that they must have a specific product they have seen right here and right now.

Whatever the different motives are for buying a product, the fact that most purchase decisions are made or influenced on the sales floor makes the point of sale an ideal marketing tool—for both the retailers and the manufacturers. There are thus several reasons why store design and visual merchandising are so important:

- Through store design, you can influence shoppers right where they make most of their buying decisions. Unlike traditional forms of marketing communication, such as media or print advertising or direct mailings, the influence that the store environment has on the consumer is immediate and three-dimensional. A store appeals to all the senses.

- In an ideal retail world, sales staff would always greet the customers, guide them through the store, discuss their needs, point out products that they might like, and in general keep them happy and in a buying mood. In reality, it is economically unfeasible for many retailers to keep the number of staff necessary to achieve all these goals. While the store environment can't entirely replace good salespeople, the right store design can lead customers through the store, provide them with information, entertain them, and even sell products to them. Best of all, your store design can do this day after day, without sick leave, training costs, or overtime pay.

- In an age of saturated markets, it is increasingly difficult for retailers to differentiate themselves from their competition. Store design can be a very effective positioning tool to do just that. By using the principles offered in this book, you can create memorable experiences for your customers that will set your store apart from the competition and create delighted, store-loyal buyers.

Store design is a fascinating, multifaceted field. Through our research and consulting work, we have gained new insights into what makes shoppers tick on a daily basis. From this research, we have distilled what we think are the most important principles. Each of these ideas is discussed in the chapters that follow. By the time you are through reading this book, you will have learned the following:

1. How shoppers navigate the store, how they search for products, and how you can make them find the products you want them to see (chapter 1)
2. Why shopper confusion kills every sale and how you can help shoppers find their way—all the way to the cash register (chapter 2)

3. How you can influence shopping behavior through such precise design factors as floors, ceilings, and store fixtures (chapter 3)
4. What the most attention-grabbing and profitable ways to present your merchandise are (chapter 4)
5. How to appeal to shopper emotions through use of colors, scents, and music (chapter 5)
6. How to make shopping memorable and fun by creating unique experiences (chapter 6)

At the end of each chapter, you find several takeaway points. They are the most important and usable insights for each of the areas we cover. The book concludes with our store design cookbook (chapter 7)—full of ready-to-serve recipes for your own store design and visual merchandising process.

CHAPTER 1

Store Layout

Understanding and Influencing How Shoppers Navigate Your Store

Consumers and marketers alike were shocked in the 1950s when journalist Vance Packard published *The Hidden Persuaders*, a book highly critical of the methods used to influence consumer behavior. In a chapter titled "Babes in Consumerland," Packard describes how consumer researchers observed women shopping in supermarkets and used this information to devise ingenious ways to "manipulate" them. Some of the in-store observations Packard described seem extremely exaggerated, stereotypical, and—from today's more focused perspective—almost comical:

> Many of these women were in such a trance that they passed by neighbors and old friends without noticing or greeting them. Some had a sort of glassy stare. They were so entranced as they wandered about the store plucking things off shelves at random that they would bump into boxes without seeing them and did not even notice the camera although in some cases their face would pass within a foot and a half of the spot where the hidden camera was clicking away.[1]

While today's consumer researchers hardly consider shoppers "in a trace" or "hypnotized" when in a store, in-store observations have remained an invaluable tool for planning and optimizing stores. They are particularly useful for planning the layout of a store. In our case we are primarily interested in the routes that shoppers (not only women but also men) take when they walk through a store (Figure 1.1).

Figure 1.1. In-store observation helps trace the routes shoppers take.

In Figure 1.2 you'll see the (partial) results of an observational study we conducted in a bookstore.[2] The lines represent the paths customers took through the store. The letters designate various product groups, such as cookbooks, travel books, stationery, and so on. While the path a single customer takes would not give you much insight, in the aggregate, typical patterns of movement do emerge. Obviously, traffic patterns in stores are not all alike. They vary depending on the layout of the store, its size, and the type of customers. For that reason, it makes good sense to conduct your own observations in a specific store to discover the problems and also the opportunities unique to that store. For example, in this bookstore there were comfortable benches that customers could use

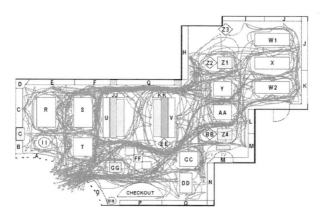

Figure 1.2. Walking patterns in a bookstore.

to sit on while browsing through the books that might have caught their interest.

As you can see, the results of this observation show that many shoppers use the reading zone (the area defined by the large benches in the middle of the store) as a shortcut to reach bookshelves located in the back of the store. In the process, they can disturb customers who are relaxing and reading books. Based on these results, we advised the management of this bookstore to slightly elevate the reading zone by adding a step to a reading platform. In this way readers could still easily access the benches, but at the same time, shoppers would be discouraged from using the reading area as a shortcut.

General Rules of Customer Traffic

While walking behavior will obviously vary from store to store, there are certain patterns that remain quite consistent. We have found them repeatedly in our studies, and they have also been reported by other marketers and consumer researchers. Let's have a look at them. We'll start right at the entrance of the store.

Transition Zone

"Caution! You are about to enter the no-spin zone," conservative talk-show host Bill O'Reilly warns viewers at the beginning of his television show. In the same way, we want to caution retailers about the transition zone in a store. This term, coined by renowned retail anthropologist Paco Underhill, refers to that area of the store immediately beyond the entrance.[3] Upon entry, customers need a short while to orient themselves in the new environment. They need to adjust to the many stimuli inside the store: the variation in lighting and temperature, the signs, the colors, and other shoppers, to mention just a few. This factor has important implications for designing the store.

The entrance is the only part of a store that every customer passes through (provided that there is only one entrance of course), and therefore many retailers and manufacturers consider it prime real estate. Nevertheless, quite the contrary is true: In the transition zone, shoppers' information-processing capabilities are so occupied with adjusting to the environment and reaching their targeted destination in the store that they only pay minimal attention to the details that surround them in this transition environment. Let's have a look at a lady entering an electronics store in Figure 1.3.

Did you see how this shopper looks straight ahead and doesn't even notice the product display to her right? She also does not notice the shopping baskets on the floor to her left. She clearly needs a few more moments to adjust to the change in her environment. Sometimes we wonder what effect a sign proclaiming, "Everything free today!" has on consumers if that sign is placed right after the entrance into the transition zone. Unfortunately, we are still searching for a client willing to let us carry out that experiment in their store.

The transition zone isn't a great place to display high-margin products or important information. This doesn't mean, however, that retailers should neglect the area right after the entrance, as it is the place to make a great first impression on shoppers and—primarily in the case of mall stores where the entrance zone is clearly visible from outside—to attract passers-by into the store. The lush fruit and vegetable departments that some supermarkets put right at their entrance are an example of this technique.

Figure 1.3. In the transition zone, the shopper looks straight ahead and doesn't notice the display to her right.

Customers Walk Counterclockwise

Have you ever noticed the direction you usually take after you have entered a store and successfully adjusted yourself to the new environment in the transition zone? While clearly not all customers are alike, many shoppers will walk counterclockwise through the store. This is a pattern that has been noticed by many consumer researchers.[4] You can also see this pattern in one of our studies. Figure 1.4 shows the interior of a supermarket. The arrow indicates the typical walking pattern we observed in the store. Notice that the diagram is indicative of the pattern where very often customers walk counterclockwise after entering a store.

It has been argued that customers tend to walk counterclockwise or to the right because in many countries they drive on the right-hand side of the road.[5] This explanation might be intuitively appealing, but it is probably wrong (e.g., consider England). We also did not observe this walking pattern in right-handed shoppers only. As research has shown, shoppers probably don't have an innate or learned predisposition to walk to the right. On the contrary, it's the store that makes them walk to the right because in most stores the entrance is on the right-hand

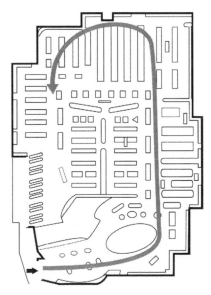

Figure 1.4. Counterclockwise movement of customers in a supermarket.

side of the storefront. Unless customers walk to the checkout area right after entering the store (which is unlikely), they are more or less forced to walk first to the back of the store on the right and then eventually turn left. In fact, recent research suggests that customers might process information better if the entrance was to the left of the store rather than the right.[6]

Customers Avoid Narrow Aisles

Stay with us in the same supermarket, and take a look at Figure 1.5. Relatively few shoppers walk in the areas that are shown in dark colors on the map, whereas the aisles that receive a lot of traffic are shown in white or light gray.

As you can see, relatively few customers enter the area that is circled because the aisles in this area are quite narrow compared to the aisles in the remainder of the store. In narrow aisles customers feel that their personal space is invaded by other shoppers. For example, they may worry that another shopper will bump into them—for this reason, this phenomenon is called "butt-brush effect"[7]—or pass at an uncomfortably close distance. It should be noted, however, that this

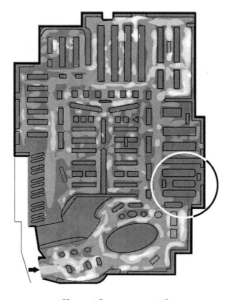

Figure 1.5. Customers will avoid narrow aisles.

is not a universal occurrence. In cultures such as the United States or the United Kingdom, people maintain a relatively large social distance, whereas in other cultures (e.g., Arab or many Latin American countries), people will stand considerably closer to each other. Consequently, aisle width is less of an issue in these countries. In the United States, on the other hand, it is essential for retailers to plan aisles that are wide enough so they signal to customers before they enter them that other shoppers will be able to pass by them comfortably and at a reasonable distance.

Shoppers Avoid Upper and Lower Floors

Research also tells us that shoppers prefer to stay on the floor where they entered the store. Generally speaking, shoppers don't like to walk up or down to another floor. Keep in mind that for some consumers, such as the disabled, obese, or elderly, moving to another floor can be downright difficult. Of course elevators and escalators (preferred over elevators by many customers) ameliorate that situation, but they do not totally eliminate this negative effect on shopper traffic. Therefore, when possible, stores should be planned to occupy a single floor (a concept you see at big-box retailers like Wal-Mart, The Home Depot, or Target). It should, however, also be noted that some shoppers tend to associate stores with more than one story as more elite, whereas one-story outlets might be seen as discount stores with less high-end merchandise.

When property comes at a premium (e.g., in downtown locations), it is not always possible for a store to occupy a single floor. In that case, the merchandise that attracts the most customers should be located on the first floor. For example, multilevel fashion stores that cater to both women and men tend to locate the ladies' department on the street level and the men's department on the second floor because in many cases women are their main customer group.

Planning the Store Layout

Now that we know how customers navigate the store, it is time to plan the optimal store layout. While there are many possibilities, some layouts are more frequently used. Let's have a look at them and analyze their advantages and their disadvantages.

Counter Store

In the days of "ye olde country store," virtually all retail outlets were counter stores. Today, however, there are relatively few stores left that employ a counter layout because this layout is incompatible with the idea of self-service. Nevertheless, there are several areas of retailing where counter service still makes sense:

- Pharmacies sell prescription drugs from behind a counter to maintain control of who receives certain medications.
- In very small stores, such as newsstands, counters are often the only practical layout.
- When shoplifting is a serious problem (e.g., where small-sized and expensive goods are sold, such as in a jewelry store), a counter layout is the best way to prevent theft.

While counter layouts are useful in these instances, they are generally not very popular in modern retailing because they are labor intensive and drastically reduce impulse purchases. Products are hidden behind counters or locked up in display cases. To a certain extent, however, this drawback can be compensated for when the sales staff is trained to use suggestive selling.[8] For a field experience in suggestive selling, just visit your local McDonald's. In this counter store, an order for a hamburger is inevitably followed by a prompt to order fries and a drink.

Forced-Path Layout

As the name implies, a forced-path layout forces the shopper to take a certain route through the store (see Figure 1.6). At least in theory, this layout is intriguing. Since the path that the shopper will take is predetermined, the layout allows the retailer to plan the shopping experience like a movie script. Once the customer is in the store, he or she follows a single path all the way to the checkout and has product contact exactly in the order predetermined by the retailer. Almost like in a Hitchcock movie, wherein Hitch sends shivers down our spines by first making us look at a woman entering a shower, then a shadow behind the curtain, then the woman's face, then the bulging shower curtain . . . you get the picture. In the store, we can use our knowledge of what the shopper will see next to influence customer behavior. Further, since the shopper passes through every aisle in the store, product contact can be maximized. This contact with many products, in turn, increases the chances for unplanned purchases.

Unfortunately, in reality, a forced-path layout is much less ideal. While it potentially maximizes product contact, it is also likely to maximize shopper irritation. How would you like to be forced to take one route and only one through a store? On the other hand, one large furniture retailer can teach us how a forced-path layout can be successfully used to guide shoppers without irritating them. That store is IKEA. At IKEA, most parts of the huge store are designed as a forced-path layout. This layout allows the company to position its products in the store in exactly the order they want shoppers to discover them and expose shoppers to a large part of the product range. What happens, however, if a customer is clearly not in a mood to stroll leisurely through IKEA's labyrinthine showrooms and instead wants to reach the checkout quickly after having selected a specific product? To deal with such quick shoppers who might easily be irritated by a forced-path layout, IKEA relies on the

Figure 1.6. Forced-path layout.

psychological principle of selective perception. People tend to perceive things more easily when the things are relevant to them than when they are irrelevant. To do this, IKEA places shortcuts at various spots in the store, which allow customers to skip parts of the store, thereby reaching the checkout much faster (see Figure 1.7). Compared to the main paths, these shortcuts are considerably narrower, and while there are signs indicating the shortcuts, they are also kept relatively inconspicuous. While the average shopper prepared to spend some time in the store would not necessarily notice the shortcuts, they will be quickly perceived by a hurried shopper looking for the exit.

Grid Layout

With a grid layout, aisles are arranged in a repetitive rectangular pattern (see Figure 1.8). It is a traffic-flow pattern traditionally favored by supermarkets, drugstores, and hardware stores. A grid layout offers several advantages:

- It allows customers to shop quickly.
- It simplifies inventory control.[9]
- Floor space is used efficiently.
- Standard fixtures can be used to display the merchandise.[10]

On the other hand, a grid layout is not particularly attractive, aesthetically pleasing, or exciting. It can look sterile and uninspiring. Further, because of the uniformity of the gondolas (freestanding store fixtures), it is not particularly easy for customers to orient themselves

Figure 1.7. Forced-path layout with shortcuts.

Figure 1.8. The grid layout.

in the store. This problem can be ameliorated, however, if an appropriate signage system is implemented and measures are taken to help customers form cognitive maps of the store in their heads (see chapter 2).

Free-Form Layout

In a free-form layout, aisles, displays, and shelves are placed in a free-flowing pattern instead of a grid. This layout has several advantages:[11]

- It enhances the atmosphere of the store and the shopping experience of the customer; the store looks less sterile and more interesting.
- Shoppers are encouraged and more likely to browse the merchandise.
- Customers feel less rushed and thus are more likely to make unplanned purchases.

There are many different possibilities for implementing a free-form layout in a store. Some of the more frequently used are the following types of store layouts:[12]

1. *Boutique layout.* The boutique layout (also called alcove or shop-in-the-shop layout) is probably the most widely used free-form layout. It is used to separate various types of merchandise sold in the store. In a boutique layout, each merchandise group is displayed in an individual, semiseparate area (see Figure 1.9).

In each of these specialty shop areas, appropriate store fixtures are then used to accentuate the theme of the area.[13] For example, in a gourmet store, there can be a cheese paradise, a wine cellar, a stone oven bakery, and so on. The interesting variety created by this layout stimulates shoppers' curiosity and is well suited for creating a unique shopping experience. The responsibility of designing and furnishing the boutiques can sit with the retailer or with the manufacturers whose merchandise is sold in the boutiques. Such a boutique, branded by a manufacturer, can be seen in Figure 1.10.

Retailers must be careful, however, when outsourcing the design of boutiques to manufacturers. As occasionally seen in some department stores, the shopper will often move from one branded boutique to another. The shopper may start at the Calvin Klein boutique and then move on to the Ralph Lauren shop, followed by the Jones New York and Tommy Hilfiger boutiques. The design of these individual boutiques may be outstanding and conducive to buying. Nevertheless, the corporate identity of the department store may become lost. After all, what is left to distinguish department store A from department store B (in terms of shopping experience) if manufacturer-branded boutiques in the two stores are nearly identical?

2. *Star layout.* In this layout, aisles are arranged in a star-like pattern. Examples of this layout can be seen in perfumeries, fashion stores, and jewelry stores (see Figure 1.11).

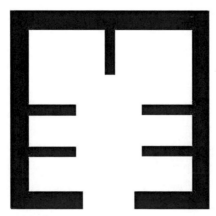

Figure 1.9. Boutique layout.

Figure 1.10. Manufacturer-branded boutique in a department store.

3. *Arena layout.* Stores using the arena layout slightly resemble amphitheaters. Often the shelves placed further back in the store are taller than the ones in the front, and these may even be placed on a pedestal. The area layout allows customers to see a large part of the product range right after entering the store. The arena layout is occasionally used in book and record stores but also in fashion stores.

Figure 1.11. Star layout used in a jewelry store.

Different layouts can also be combined. An international super-market chain, for example, has combined the classical grid layout traditionally found in supermarkets with a free-form layout (see Figure 1.12). Perhaps you have heard about the right brain–left brain theory, which can relate to this type of store layout. Our brain consists of two hemispheres. While this statement is somewhat of a generalization, the left side of our brain seems to be more involved in linear reason-ing, whereas the right hemisphere appears to play an important role in creativity. This type of supermarket layout is also divided into two hemispheres.

The left side of the store (about one half of the total floor space) is where "boring" items such as frozen food, garbage bags, and deter-gents are sold in a grid layout. The right side of the store, on the other hand, employs a free-form layout. This part of the store looks like a luscious marketplace and is where produce, wine, cheese, and a wide variety of deli items are sold. Unlike the functional left side of the store, the right side of the store appeals to hedonic shoppers who enjoy sampling the smorgasbord of delicacies that are sold on the premises.

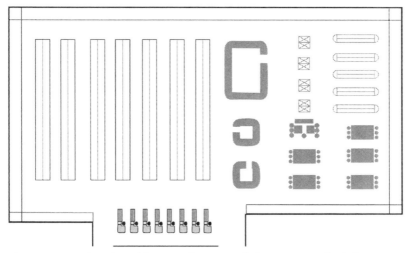

Figure 1.12. Combined layout: Functional shopping on the left, hedonic shopping on the right.

The Loop: Guiding the Shopper Through the Store

Wouldn't it be nice if you could take your customers by the hand and guide each one through your store while pointing out all the great products you would like them to consider buying? Most people, however, would not particularly enjoy having a stranger grab their hand and drag them through a store. But there is another way to achieve a similar result: Let the store do it for you. Have a central path that leads shoppers through the store and lets them look at many different departments or product areas. Just as Dorothy in *The Wizard of Oz* followed the yellow brick road all the way to the Emerald City, this path leads your customers from the entrance through the store on the road you want them to take all the way to checkout.

In a store, this yellow brick road is called a loop. While some authors maintain that a store containing a loop is a specific form of layout (and call it a "racetrack layout"), we think that a loop can be implemented in most layouts, and it can be a more or less prominent feature of the store. A loop may be very pronounced in a fashion store and less so in a grocery retail store. Nevertheless, when planning the store layout, it should always be clear what main path we desire shoppers to take when navigating our store. Loops are particularly useful in larger stores of over 5,000 square feet, where encouraging shoppers to explore different parts of the store is more difficult than it would be in smaller retail outlets.[14]

The loop must be clearly visible and also communicate to customers that it is the best and easiest approach to traversing the store. Making the loop visible can be achieved in several ways:

- Marking the loop on the floor in a different color
- Guiding customers along the loop via additional lighting on the ceiling
- Using a different flooring material to mark the loop

In some stores, loops are indicated by lines on the floor. These clearly mark the loops and also prevent store clerks from placing merchandise in the floor space reserved for the walking loop. Nevertheless, we advise against this approach because the lines could be perceived as a psychological barrier by some customers. After all, the loop is supposed to guide customers through the store, but customers must always feel comfortable about stepping away from the loop to explore products in other areas of the store.

It is not enough to make the loop visible. If you want to ensure that your customers follow the loop all the way through the store, it is necessary to place focus points along the loop (Figure 1.13). These are, in effect, landmarks that will attract customer attention. Whenever shoppers reach a focus point, another focus point should already be in their field of vision. In a sense, you should always reward shoppers for following the loop by providing them with interesting sights along the way. If done right, these focus points will serve as bread crumbs for customers to follow, as in the story of Hansel and Gretel, all the way to the cash register.

Where to Place Merchandise and How Shoppers Search for Products

Imagine you are leisurely shopping at a department store. All of a sudden, you encounter an otherwise normal-looking fellow shopper wearing

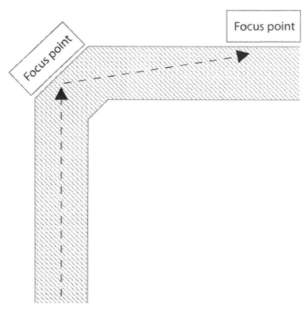

Figure 1.13. Focus points will lead the shopper along the loop.

a strange device attached to a baseball cap (see Figure 1.14). A cable runs from the device to a backpack the stranger carries on his shoulder. What at first glance may appear like an alien from another planet is in fact a research participant who is helping us study where shoppers look while in the store. The device he is wearing is an eye tracker. It precisely records the eye movement of the shopper. These eye movements are superimposed on a video of the store from a notebook computer hidden in the person's backpack.

An eye tracker records both a person's eye movements (called saccades) and where the eye stops (fixations). Our eyes move rapidly, constantly scanning our environment for new visual information. While the eye moves, the person is virtually blind—that is, no information is registered. We don't notice this, however, because of the speed at which our eyes *do* move— saccades last for only 20 to 40 milliseconds! It is the eye fixations that consumer researchers are really interested in. When the eyes remain still for at least ¼ to ½ second, the brain will process information received by the eye.[15] Measuring these fixations allows us to determine which visual stimuli in the store attract and hold the shopper's attention. In Figure 1.15 you can see one shopper's gaze path while searching for a detergent on a shelf. The circles indicate the shopper's fixations. Larger circles indicate longer

Figure 1.14. A shopper wearing an eye tracker.

Figure 1.15. A shopper's gaze while searching for a product.

fixations on a visual stimulus (e.g., a particular product) than the smaller circles. The bold circle shows the shopper's current fixation.

Obviously, shoppers don't all look at the same spots in a store when shopping. Consumer researchers have known for a long time that shoppers' individual differences and, in particular, their various interests influence which stimuli they pay attention to and which they don't. Nevertheless, eye-tracking research as well as traditional observation of shoppers has provided us with useful insights into what attracts customers' attention.

Shelf Zones: Eye Level Is Buy Level

Have you ever heard the old retail adage "eye level is buy level"? While it is almost a cliché, it still holds true. Products placed at the shoppers' eye level tend to sell significantly better than products at other heights on the shelf because products at eye level receive more attention than products placed either above or below. This principle is so powerful you can even use it in your own fridge! Nutritional experts suggest placing healthy foods at eye level in the refrigerator.[16] So the next time you open the door to your fridge, your strategically placed broccoli will catch your attention immediately (before your eyes start wandering to the cupcakes at the bottom). Let's go back to the store, though, and see how retail experts divide shelve space into four distinct, vertical zones (Figure 1.16):

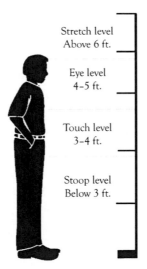

Figure 1.16. The four vertical shelf zones.

- *Stretch level* (> 6 ft.). This is one of the less valuable shelf zones. Shelves on the stretch level receive relatively little attention by shoppers. Furthermore, only lightweight products should be placed in this zone to prevent possible injuries. Some modern store fixtures have done away with shelves on the stretch level altogether. This decision has the advantage that the store seems airier and less crowded. Because the shelves are shorter, the shoppers' sight is also not blocked. This view can induce more shoppers to visit the back of the store. In spite of these developments, many stores do still have tall shelves because the space *above* the stretch level is used for inventory.
- *Eye level* (4–5 ft.). Shoppers can only buy what they see, and what is in their field of vision receives the most attention. Perceptive retailers have known for a long time that products displayed at eye level sell best. This assumption has received support from research studies using eye-tracking technology. One study found that products placed at eye level received 35% greater attention than those on a lower shelf.[17] This finding also corresponds with our own in-store observations. It should be pointed out, however, that placing eye level at between 4 and 5 ft. is only an approximation. A person's peripheral vision extends 30° from

their central focus point in all directions.[18] Consequently, the
further away shoppers stand from a shelf, the wider the eye-level
zone will extend. When selling products aimed at children, the
eye-level zone obviously is located further down on the shelf.
Nevertheless, these basic findings hold true for children as well.
As our research has shown, children are considerably more likely
to request product purchases from their parents for products
placed at their own lower eye level.[19] Eye level is the ideal zone
for placing products with a high profit margin.

- *Touch level* (3–4 ft.). The touch level is located approximately at
the shopper's waist height. Products placed in this zone receive
more attention than products at the stretch level and stoop level
but also receive somewhat less attention than products at eye level.
It is still a desirable zone, however, for placing high-profit items.

- *Stoop level* (< 3 ft.). Shoppers don't like to bend down or—
in the case of elderly or disabled people—may be unable to
bend down. Furthermore, the stoop level is not usually in
most shoppers' fields of vision while walking through a store.
Consequently, the stoop level is retailing's equivalent of the
boondocks, where low-margin merchandise finds its place.
Heavy products are also placed in this shelf zone for safety
reasons and easier selection by customers.

It should be noted that the placement of products on different vertical
shelf zones does not only affect perception. There is evidence that consumers also evaluate products differently depending on which shelf they are
placed on. As we already know, products placed both at eye level and at
touch level receive more attention than products located either above or
below these two levels. These two zones differ, however, with respect to how
favorably customers judge the brands they find there. In an experiment, it
was shown that brands placed on a higher shelf (eye level) were evaluated
better than brands placed on a lower shelf (touch level), irrespective of the
actual brands.[20] Apparently, shoppers have (implicitly) learned over time
that retailers tend to give the top positions on the shelf to the top brands.

At this point you may be wondering if there is also an optimal horizontal shelf position. After all, it would be useful to know if products
receive more attention if they are placed near the center or at peripheral

positions of the shelf. Horizontal shelf zones have also been identified. Merchandise at the center of a shelf appears to receive the greatest
visual attention by shoppers.[21] This placement assumes, of course, that
the shopper stands directly in front of the center of the shelf, which in
most cases is not very likely. While shoppers may pay more attention to
the middle of a shelf in some situations, a lot seems to depend on where
in the store the shelf is located and from which direction customers
approach the shelf. For example, many shoppers don't walk through an
entire aisle (particularly if the aisles are very long). Instead, they may
just enter the aisle, search for a particular product, and then leave the
aisle where they entered. If many consumers enter the aisle from the
same direction, products placed on shelves close to the entrance of the
aisle are in a great selling spot because more shoppers pass this section
of the shelf than any other (and may consequently notice these products more often).

How Customers Search for Products on the Shelves

As we have seen, the best spot on a shelf is not that easy to determine. We do know, however, how customers search for products on
shelves. Primarily, shoppers search horizontally. After all, the majority
of our eye muscles are made for horizontal movement.[22] Imagine for a
moment a shopper searching for AAA batteries on a shelf (see Figure
1.17). Typically, this shopper will first scan the shelf horizontally as she

Figure 1.17. Shoppers scan shelves mostly horizontally.

walks down the aisle: light bulbs . . . extension cords . . . chargers . . . Aha! Batteries. Only after she has found batteries will she start scanning the shelf vertically for the specific type or brand of battery she is looking for.

This sequence—first horizontal scanning for merchandise groups, then vertical scanning for specific brands or products—has important implications for how merchandise should be arranged on shelves. To take advantage of shoppers' search patterns, similar products should be arranged in vertical blocks and not horizontal blocks. If product blocks are arranged horizontally, shoppers often have problems finding what they are looking for because of their vertical search pattern. Therefore, don't put cameras on the top shelf, camcorders on the shelf below, and so on. Instead, build a vertical block for cameras, followed by a vertical block for camcorders, and so on (see Figure 1.18).

Have a look at Figure 1.19. On this shelf displaying accessories for electric shavers, shoppers would have to search vertically to find the type of product they want because the different types of accessories are arranged horizontally rather than vertically. Since shoppers primarily scan horizontally (until they find the desired product category), many will have a hard time finding what they need and may simply move on.

There are two ways to design vertical blocks:

1. *Product blocks.* Merchandise is grouped by product category. For example, one vertical block contains soaps, whereas another one contains shampoos.

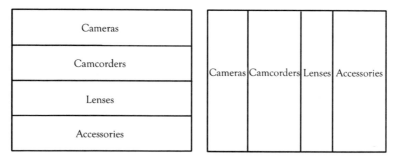

Figure 1.18. Horizontal (left) versus vertical blocks (right).

Figure 1.19. *Grouping product categories horizontally forces shoppers to scan vertically to find an item, which they hate to do.*

2. *Brand blocks.* Merchandise is grouped by brands. For example, one vertical block contains all Ivory products, another block all Dove products, and a third block all Palmolive products.

A store doesn't only consist of shelves, though. There are other store fixtures and in-store media that shoppers look at as well. One study investigated what percentage of customers notices various fixtures and in-store media.[23] The results were as follows:

- End aisle displays: 100%
- Free-standing product display racks: 100%
- Display bins: 97%
- Shelf ads: 62%
- Coupon dispensers: 50%

As you can see, end aisle displays, often called "end caps," are noticed by every shopper. In addition, this study found that end caps are noticed more often per shopping trip (on average 16 times, as opposed to only 9 times for product displays or 4 times for display bins). This makes them true attention hot spots, particularly if they are located in the front sections of a store where most customers will pass by.[24] Consequently, retailers use them for secondary placements.

In a secondary placement, particularly profitable merchandise is displayed not only in its regular place on the shelf but also a second or even a third time in places where it will be noticed by many shoppers. Particularly, products that have a potential to lead to impulse purchases are placed in end caps. So on a shopping trip to the supermarket, we may try to fastidiously avoid the snack food aisle to resist the temptation to buy fattening potato chips but to no avail because these chips also lurk at an end cap on our way to the produce department.

If you insist, however, on making us buy the potato chips in your store, let us (a bit unwillingly) share with you the secret of several other high-selling zones in the store. What all of these hot spots have in common is that they grab shopper attention:

- The area in front of the checkout where customers have to wait
- Display bins blocking the shoppers' path
- Areas next to elevators and escalators where shoppers pause

Just make sure not to place the potato chips (or other items you want us to buy) in areas that shoppers avoid: narrow aisles, dead ends—even if the empty space may be tempting for you to use, these chips would never tempt us to go into those areas—and never ever after checkout. Only shoplifters pay attention to products displayed after the checkout.

Takeaway Points

Here are the most important takeaway points from this chapter:

- To plan the optimal store layout, you need to know how shoppers move through your store.
- While no two stores are exactly alike, certain general patterns of how shoppers navigate a shopping environment can be identified. Taking these patterns into consideration when planning a store layout will improve shopper satisfaction and store profitability.
- Different layouts can be identified. When choosing one of these layouts, consider various factors, such as efficiency, ease

of orientation, and the potential for a layout to make shopping fun for the consumer.

- While a forced-path layout encourages shopper contact with the merchandise, be careful not to alienate customers by forcing their route. More subtle approaches to influence shoppers may often be more effective.
- No matter what layout you choose, specify the loop or the main path you would like customers to take through the store. Then think of ways to entice your customers to follow the loop all the way through the store.
- Consider tracking eye movements to find out exactly where shoppers look when they are in your store. Remember that shoppers can only buy what they see.
- Shoppers scan shelves mostly horizontally. Consequently, similar products should be arranged in vertical blocks.
- Eye level is buy level. Optimize both vertical and horizontal shelf placement to good advantage.
- Put your high-margin products in the top-selling zones in the store. While you need a full assortment so that customers will visit your store, once customers are in the store, the high-margin items should be glaringly conspicuous.

CHAPTER 2

Where Am I?

Helping Shopper Orientation in Your Store

One of the most basic principles of store design is that consumers desire order in their world. While customers also want a friendly staff, attractive surroundings, and so forth, all of these are of little value if the shopper feels overwhelmed by the store. This can easily happen because today most stores are self-service stores. Particularly in large retail spaces, consumers can easily lose track of their surroundings. Just imagine stores like Wal-Mart Supercenters, which are an average size of 197,000 square feet.[1] Isn't it easy to get lost and confused in such vast spaces? But even in smaller stores, consumers can feel lost.

The Effects of Shoppers Losing Their Orientation in the Store

A person's locus of control is the extent to which a person feels in control. A person rating high on internal locus of control is convinced that he can control his environment, whereas a person whose locus of control is primarily external feels that the environment is controlling him. On the one hand, locus of control is a personality trait. Perhaps you know people you would describe as go-getters. These are individuals who rate high on internal locus of control. However, even these individuals can at times feel helpless when put in an unfamiliar or confusing environment. Just imagine looking for a motel late at night in a foreign country where you don't speak the language. While the shopping situation is less dramatic, a consumer in a large store can similarly feel confused and disoriented. Most often this happens when consumers search for a long time to find a particular product and can't find it.

When consumers feel that they are no longer in control of their environment, there is anger and severe dissatisfaction expressed toward the store. This negativity, in turn, leads to several unfortunate effects on consumer behavior:

- Consumers spend less time in the store.
- They become more critical in their evaluation of the merchandise.
- They are less likely to make unplanned purchases.
- Store loyalty is negatively impacted.

Therefore, it is crucial for retailers to help their shoppers orient themselves in their stores. You will now learn how to accomplish this task.

Cognitive Maps Can Put Your Customers Back on Track

If we want to improve shopper orientation in your store, we must first understand how consumers read their environment and what clues they use to find their way around a shopping environment. Therefore, let's have a look into the shopper's mind. People store mental representations of their environment in their heads. These mental representations are called cognitive maps.[2] The mental maps in people's heads look, however, quite different from street maps or city maps. Our minds store the information we need for finding our way very selectively. What are the features that help us read the environment?

To find out, architect and city planner Kevin Lynch asked volunteers in several American cities, including Los Angeles and Boston, to draw maps of their cities. He found that only a very limited number of a city's features consistently appeared in most of these cognitive maps. They were paths, nodes, districts, edges, and landmarks.[3] These are the same features consumers use to orient themselves in stores and service environments. Let's take a closer look at them.

Paths

Paths are the main arteries of a city, and they also lead people through a store. To help customers navigate a store, there must be clear paths, such as the one you can see in Figure 2.1. Customers will find their way around more easily when corridors leading through the store are clearly distinguishable as main or secondary paths.

Nodes

Nodes are places where people congregate. Often a node is created where paths intersect, such as in a town square. In a store, nodes are found at the intersection of aisles.

Districts

Every city has districts that have a unique feel. Think of Chinatown, the red light district, downtown, and so on. When you move from one district to another, you notice the change. The houses look different, the streets and alleys are narrower, and the landscaping changes. In a store, parts of the

Figure 2.1. A clearly visible, broad path improves shopper orientation in a store.

store where similar merchandise is displayed that are decorated uniquely will be perceived as districts and consequently help provide shoppers with positive orientation.

Edges

Edges are barriers such as rivers, fences, walls, and railroad tracks. They also help customers find their way through a city. In stores you can find barriers that separate different sections, such as the music and movies section in a bookstore. Consumer researchers have found that supermarket shoppers find it easier to remember the position of products in a store if the products are located on the edges of the store rather than in the middle aisles.[4] This concept is shown in Figure 2.2, where little dots represent product with locations correctly identified by customers.

Landmarks

Features in an environment that are large or look unique are called landmarks. Landmarks attract attention and are usually recognized by many people.[5] Every city has such landmarks. For example, in New York City you find the arch in Washington Square, the Statue of Liberty, the Brooklyn Bridge, and many more. Landmarks (on a smaller scale) can also be

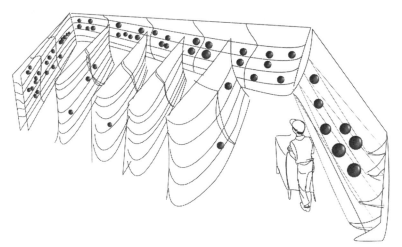

Figure 2.2. Shoppers remember products placed in peripheral aisles better than products placed in central aisles.

Figure 2.3. A fountain as a landmark in a fashion store.

found in stores, such as the fountain in Figure 2.3, which attracts shoppers' attention when walking through a fashion store. Stores and service facilities can even be landmarks in their own right, such as the Tail o' the Pup hot dog stand in Los Angeles, a prime example of 1950s mimetic architecture.

Figure 2.4. A hot dog stand as a recognizable landmark.

Incorporating the knowledge derived from the study of cognitive maps can significantly improve consumer orientation in a store or service environment and make the shopping experience more pleasurable.[6] This fact has long been known by those "imagineers" who design theme parks for the Walt Disney Corporation. Can you find all the elements of a cognitive map in this drawing that depicts Disney's Magic Kingdom theme park (Figure 2.5)?

There are clear paths throughout the park. The first one, Main Street USA, starts right at the entrance and leads us toward the center of the Magic Kingdom, where Cinderella's Castle, the theme park's main landmark, is located. In front of the castle is one of many central squares, a node. From there, paths lead to the various "lands": Adventureland, Frontierland, Futureland, and so on. Each of these districts is uniquely themed and contains a landmark that exemplifies that land and draws visitors further into the park. Waterways are used to separate the districts from each another. Together with hedges and walls, they become the edges, which further improve visitor orientation in the park.

Now let's have a look at how we can we can implement the insights from cognitive maps in our store. If you want to apply the

Figure 2.5. Elements of cognitive maps found at Disney's Magic Kingdom.

principles of cognitive maps to store design, there are several things you can do:

- First and foremost, there should be clearly visible paths leading through the store. Remove any clutter from the aisles. We have seen many stores where merchandise oozes onto the aisles. Unfortunately, this intrusion severely impedes shopper navigation in the store. An example of this problem can be seen in Figure 2.6. In this picture, also note the bulky columns blocking both the aisles and also the merchandise on the shelves. For a manufacturer, having a product placed on a shelf behind both a column and the merchandise in the aisle must feel like the retail equivalent of hell. One wonders if this positioning is punishment for not paying a slotting fee demanded by the retailer. When designing paths leading through your store, also pay attention to the width of the different aisles. The width of the aisles serves as an indication to shoppers about which aisles are the main roads and which ones are only secondary routes.
- Group similar merchandise together, and break up heterogeneous products. Doing so will make consumers perceive

Figure 2.6. Merchandise and columns blocking the shoppers' path.

different areas in the store as districts and help them to orient themselves. Districts can be formed by using shelves, carpeting, decorations, and colors. For example, the wine section in a supermarket could become a unique district by using wood shelves (in contrast to the metal shelves used elsewhere in the store) and a wooden floor. In a bookstore, the children's section can also become a unique district using a brighter color scheme than found in the rest of the store, placing children's furniture in that section, and so on.

• Landmarks can be used in all of these districts. They help shopper orientation and also induce shoppers to further explore the store because people in a store tend to walk toward landmarks. As an example, in the fruit and vegetable section of a supermarket, a large artificial fruit tree can serve as a landmark. In an electronics store, a large video wall can signal to shoppers where the TV sets are sold. When physical landmarks are difficult to implement, large pictures could serve as landmarks. This is typical in a building supply store (Figure 2.7), where pictures of people carrying out various construction jobs are used as landmarks.

Figure 2.7. Large pictures can serve as landmarks.

Signage Systems Guide Shoppers Through the Store

The thoughtful and creative implementation of the features contained in cognitive maps is a great way to improve customer orientation in a store. There are, however, other measures you can take to help your customers find their way around the store, including signage systems and maps.

Not every signage system works, however. Unclear and confusing signs will hinder rather than help consumers in finding their way. Good signage systems incorporate some or all of the following features.[7]

Visibility

Signs must stand out and be visible. While from an architectural or artistic point of view, it might be desirable if signs harmonize or blend in with the environment, signs are only helpful to customers if they can be clearly and easily seen. It is of particular importance that signs are at an appropriate height to be noticed by customers. Placing signs too high is one of the most frequent signage mistakes we see in the stores we analyze.

Quantity

Less is definitely more as far as signage goes. Indeed, using too many signs can lead to information overload. Also, you should limit the number of messages per sign. Ideally, use one message per sign. Limiting the number of signs visible to a consumer at any one time and the number of messages on a sign is necessary because of the severe capacity constraints of the consumer's information-processing system. Have you ever heard of the magic number seven? That's approximately how many items we are able to keep in our short-term memory at any one time.[8] It is for this reason that phone numbers (in the United States) are limited to seven digits (excluding the area code). In fact, many consumers may only be able to keep only three or four pieces of information in their short-term memories where thinking actually occurs. As a consequence, too many signs seen at any one time may confuse rather than guide the shopper (see Figure 2.8).

Figure 2.8. Don't confuse a shopper with too many signs.

Legibility

The message on the sign must be easy to read. This clarity is determined by the distance between the sign and the consumer, the illumination in the room, the font used on the sign, and the contrast between the background and the letters or symbols on the sign. There are several guidelines you can follow to make signs more legible to shoppers:

- Serif fonts (fonts containing small lines at the end of letters) are more legible in books and magazines, but sans-serif fonts appear to be more legible on signs (see Figure 2.9).
- A mixture of capitals and lower-case letters is more legible than all caps. When both upper- and lower-case text is used, even people with vision impairment or learning disabilities may still

Sans-serif fonts	Serif fonts
Fitting rooms	Fitting rooms
Fitting rooms	**Fitting rooms**
Fitting rooms	Fitting rooms

Figure 2.9. Examples of sans-serif and serif fonts. Sans-serif fonts are more legible on signs.

be able to recognize the shape of the words. For single word signs (EXIT, RESTROOM), all caps are acceptable.[9] The color of the font and the background also influences legibility: Black letters on a yellow or white background are most legible.[10] No matter what colors you use on a sign, high contrast between the color of the font and the color of the background is crucial for legibility.

Intelligibility

Even if signs are visible and legible, they may still not be helpful to customers if customers don't understand the message. This lack of understanding can be due to the language used to convey the message. For that reason, in the United States, in areas with a large Hispanic population, store signs are often bilingual, presented in English and Spanish. In northern Vermont and New Hampshire, signs are often in both English and French because Canada is so close. When designing signs, one must also consider illiterate and functionally illiterate consumers. It is estimated that 20% of the U.S. population is functionally illiterate.[11] Their reading ability is very limited (below that of a 5th grader). Consequently, simple words should be used on signs whenever possible and—as we will see later—it is always advisable to complement text with pictures

Color coding is another method used to make signs more intelligible. Various colors can help to identify different sections of a store or emphasize particular signs. For example, in many airports, all signs leading to the exit are color coded in yellow, whereas signs leading to the gates are color coded in green.

Obviously, an important consideration when implementing a signage system in a store or a service environment is cost. In particular, a signage system should be flexible. When parts of a store or merchandise changes, you should be able to change related signs without incurring significant costs. Flexibility is particularly important in the service business. For example, in a movie theater or conference center, it is important to easily and quickly change signs that lead customers to different rooms for different movies or meetings.[12] For this reason electronic screens have become widely used in these settings.

We discovered another important principle of signage when we conducted a study to optimize the signage system of a large supermarket chain for elderly consumers. In this experiment, we asked senior citizens to search for several products in the store and measured how long it took them to find all of them. To make their task easier, we put signs in each aisle that had both a verbal description of the products found in the aisle and a picture of a typical product. For example a sign would read "snacks" and simultaneously display a pack of potato chips. We noticed that seniors found the requested products significantly quicker when the information on the sign was presented in both verbal and pictorial form than when we used traditional text-only signs. Most interestingly, the advantage of signs with both words and pictures also extended to young consumers. This finding can be explained by the dual-processing theory: Consumers mentally process and retrieve stimuli more easily and efficiently when the stimuli are presented in both verbal and pictorial form.[13] In fact, in many ways, pictures are superior to verbal signs because they tend to be more easily perceived, processed, and retrieved.[14] Consequently, it is advisable to incorporate pictures in a store's signage system like the ones seen in Figure 2.10.

Figure 2.10. Combination of text and pictures in a store sign.

Store Maps

Maps are another way to help customers find their way around. The type of map most commonly found in stores, shopping malls, and service facilities is the "you-are-here" map. These maps depict the environment where the customer is currently located. An arrow or circle indicates that exact location. Such a map can be seen in Figure 2.11.

The problem with you-are-here maps is that they are often confusing to customers. The confusion derives from the fact that two important environmental psychology principles, structure matching and orientation, are frequently neglected when designing or positioning these maps.[15]

Structure matching implies that the map reflects the store or service environment it represents. To improve structure matching, these maps should use labels that resemble images found in the setting, such as logos (e.g., notice the IKEA logo in Figure 2.11). Furthermore, the you-are-here symbol should point to the customer's exact location, not just state it.

The orientation principle states that whatever is in front of the consumer must be at the top of the map. In other words, "up" on the map must relate to "straight ahead" in the environment. This is illustrated

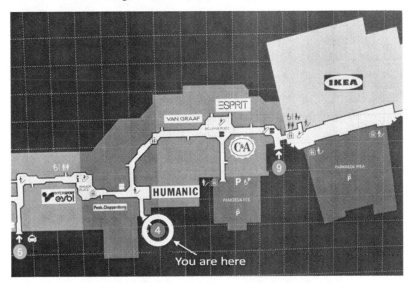

Figure 2.11. A typical you-are-here map in a shopping mall.

in Figure 2.12 and Figure 2.13, which show a correct and an incorrect orientation of a you-are-here map. In Figure 2.12 you can see that the map shows on top what the shopper sees when he looks straight ahead (correct orientation). In Figure 2.13 the map also correctly represents the environment surrounding the shopper, but it is confusing to most people because the arrow points to the left. Scouts, pilots, and soldiers probably wouldn't have a problem with this map, but the average shopper (and this includes us, the authors) would.

Positive Ways to Facilitate Orientation in a Store

You have implemented the principles of cognitive maps, come up with logical and consistent signage systems, and perhaps even provided you-are-here maps. What else can you do to ensure that shoppers feel in control rather than disoriented? Here are a few suggestions.

Orient the Layout of the Store on Shoppers' Scripts

Consumers frequently follow scripts when shopping. A script is a cognitive sequence of behaviors.[16] In a sense it is like a movie script that sits in our head. For example, by analyzing consumers' shopping lists, we have found that the shoppers in a particular supermarket often organized their shopping activities by meals. First they looked for breakfast items, then groceries for lunch, and then dinner items. Frozen food usually was bought right before heading to the checkout. In other stores, very different scripts will influence the sequence of shopping activities, but analyzing consumers' brain scripts and organizing merchandise according to them may help you facilitate your shoppers' orientation in the store.

Color Coding

We have already explored how color coding can improve the intelligibility of signs. Color coding isn't limited to signs, however. You can also color code different departments, merchandise groups, or store levels.

Figure 2.12. Correct orientation of a you-are-here map.

Figure 2.13. A confusing you-are-here map that violates the orientation principle.

Directional Signs on Walls and the Floor

Most signage systems employ overhead signs. Nevertheless, the walls and the floor can also be used to direct shoppers. For example, large hospitals often use colored lines on the walls to guide patients and visitors to different departments. On the floor, a line or stylized footprints can lead shoppers to a special offer. In this context we have found that when a red line on the floor of a university building led to one of several soda machines, sales at that particular soda machine increased significantly over those of the other machines. Floor lines or footprints should not be overused, however. Otherwise they might lose the element of surprise and, consequently, their effectiveness.

Takeaway Points

Here are the most important takeaway points from this chapter:

- It is crucial to customer satisfaction that shoppers easily navigate a store. If shoppers feel that they are dominated by the store environment, they will become frustrated and angry.
- While we like customers to spend a long time in a store, only quality time will lead to the all-important unplanned purchase. If shoppers spend time in the store because they can't find the merchandise they want, that won't help at all.
- Customers store cognitive maps in their brains that help them navigate the store. If you include the elements that most people include in their own cognitive maps in the design of your store, you will improve shopper orientation. Elements like landmarks and districts also make a store more appealing and interesting.
- A well-planned signage system can significantly improve shopper orientation.
- Less is more: There should be only one message per sign.
- Less is more: To avoid information overload, there should be as few signs as possible in a store.

- Combine text with pictures. This will make a message easier to process for everyone, and you can also reach shoppers who are functionally illiterate or don't speak English.
- You-are-here maps can complement a good signage system, but only if the map is oriented correctly.
- Organizing the merchandise according to shoppers' brain scripts facilitates orientation.

CHAPTER 3

Store Design Factors

Looking Good From Store Front to Store Back

"We shape our buildings and our buildings shape us."[1] This adage, attributed to Winston Churchill, refers to the fact that buildings (in our case, stores) influence people—a common theme of this book. Sometimes, however, the store literally shapes the customers and their shopping choices. Such was the case for Jenna, a fashion-conscious shopper who tried on a pair of jeans in the fitting room of an upscale fashion store. When she looked at herself in the oversized mirrors, she was very pleased with her choice. The jeans made her look slim and trim (see Figure 3.1). Unfortunately, when she tried on the same jeans at home, she looked slightly less slim. How can that be? Well, Jenna, as we know from the title of an old Agatha Christie mystery, "They do it with mirrors" (and the proper light).

Distorting mirrors are just one of the fascinating topics we cover in the following pages. Unlike the previous chapter where we focused on atmospheric factors, here you will learn about the physical, tangible

Figure 3.1. Store mirrors can be treacherous.

aspects of a store. In general, these tangible elements can be divided into exterior design factors (such as windows or walls) and interior design elements (such as floor covering, displays, and those mirrors; see Figure 3.2).

Exterior Design: First Impressions Count

Let's start with the exterior design factors. The first impression a shopper gets of your store is exterior design, also referred to as the storefront. Most customers decide whether to enter a store or not within a few seconds of observation. Therefore the main aim of exterior design is first to attract a customer's attention and then convey a certain image that entices that customer into the store. Flagship stores spend huge amounts of money on their storefronts to brand their stores. Since these stores are usually between five and eight times larger than other retail stores, already by virtue of large storefronts, they will attract many customers. In addition, they are often located in high-end shopping districts and use premises that are significant to the community, such as former factories, marketplaces, or historical landmarks.[2] Not every store can be a flagship store, however.

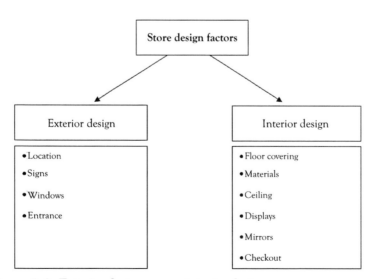

Figure 3.2. Exterior design versus interior design.

Nevertheless, there are options to impress and attract shoppers who notice the exterior of a store.

To create an appealing storefront, the exterior should be coherent with the store's interior theme. For example, Harris Teeter, a supermarket in Virginia Beach, Virginia, conveys their farmers' market theme even in their exterior design by using rural forms, materials, and details. Shoppers standing in front of this store feel like they are in a rural area, although the shop is located in the middle of suburbia. The open, gabled roof and the overall building silhouette remind consumers of rustic farming architecture. Exterior walls are painted with alternating stripe patterns in combination with walls featuring split-faced blocks, and the use of traditional materials like galvanized metal, distressed blocks, and painted structural steel conveys a rural image that communicates to its prospective customers that delightfully fresh and natural food is for sale inside.[3] Several factors can contribute to a successful exterior store design, such as Harris Teeter's. These will be discussed in the next sections.

Where Should the Store Be Located?

Even if it is a somewhat tired cliché, "location, location, location" still is one of most important success factors in retailing. There is a lot of truth to the adage. No matter whether a store is planned for a shopping mall, a strip mall, or the central business district, the amount of pedestrian or vehicle customer traffic must be considered when choosing the location. Even within a shopping mall, not all locations provide the desired traffic. Stores located in side corridors or (contrary to popular opinion) near mall entrances are typically less frequented than stores at the center of a mall. When selecting a store location in a shopping mall, the rental price will usually indicate how good that location actually is—or at least how good the mall management considers the location to be. In most modern shopping malls, traffic is continuously measured, usually by devices installed at or above entrances. Nevertheless, before choosing a location, store management should visit a mall numerous times to check out where different entertainment activities happen to get a full picture about the number of people passing the intended location.[4] In addition, there are other general guidelines to follow when you're selecting a mall location for your store:[5]

- *Escalators.* Being close to all the mall's central escalators is a great place for many stores. However, not all locations near an escalator will bring you the desired attention from customers. Instead, direction matters. Locate your store near the top of an up escalator or the bottom of a down escalator. A store located at the top of a down escalator will be at risk of being only perceived as the entrance point to the escalator.
- *Anchors.* Anchor stores, such as a department stores or super-markets, are important customer magnets for shopping centers overall. However, it is not advantageous for an individual store to be located too close to an anchor store. Within about 50 feet of an anchor store, shoppers become often transfixed by the anchor and don't pay much attention to stores located within that space.
- *Wells.* In retail jargon, a well refers to an opening on the upper level of a shopping mall that creates a gallery. It lets shoppers have a view of the lower level of the shopping mall. This opening divides customer traffic into two lanes (see Figure 3.3). For instance, if shoppers decide to take the right lane, and your store is located at the left lane, customers will have to walk down the whole gallery to get to your store. It is a better idea to locate your store on either end of the gallery so shoppers can quickly cross over to your store.

Figure 3.3. Traffic flow is divided into two lines at a well.

- *Longest, continuous path.* If the shopping mall consists of a long hallway of stores, with an anchor store on both ends, all locations on this hallway will be good. In contrast, if the mall consists of several corridors and courts, the best location will be found on the longest path of the mall.
- *Neighborhood.* A store should be located among stores that attract the same target group as the planned store. For example, an exclusive shoe boutique should not consider a location next to a discount, low-cost shoe outlet but instead look to locate next to an exclusive fashion store. Don't fear your competition: Use it. Even in the centuries-old bazaars of Egypt and Turkey, most of the carpet stores are in one part of the bazaar, while the stores selling spices and incense congregate in another section. This agglomeration of similar stores attracts shoppers who are in the market for similar products because they know the specific places where they can find a large selection of what they want. This marketing wisdom is hard to argue against. And another tried-and-true tip for choosing a location is that, in general, a good location for many stores is next to food vendors. Popcorn and ice cream will bring people to even the most undesirable locations.[6]

A successful store need not necessarily be located in a mall. Street stores in urban locations, such as a central business district or a main street, provide several advantages, too. Nevertheless, that picture is slightly different. Usually, shoppers drive to a mall to go shopping. In the city, there are many pedestrians who do not intend to actually shop. However, there are several ways for a street store to still attract shoppers.

Let's imagine a pedestrian walking down the street, lost in thought, directing her eyes to the ground. It is definitely a challenge for a store to attract this person. In this situation, signs or a beautiful store window will not be noticed. Nevertheless, there is another way to get that customer's attention: Communicate through the pavement in front of the store. This can be done with different materials, distinct colors, or even by putting the company's logo on the pavement. Additionally (or if zoning laws prohibit embellishment of the pavement), you can take several other actions to attract the attention of pedestrians passing your store:[7]

- *Flowers.* If trees are in front of the store, think of planting flowers around the tree. They will not only serve as an eye-catcher but also contribute a pleasant atmosphere to your store's surroundings.
- *Lights.* While it has become common to decorate trees during the holiday season, more and more stores use this tool to attract customers all year round. After all, isn't there always a time to celebrate—and shop?
- *Benches.* Place benches in front of the store, but always facing the store, never the other direction. Anyone taking a seat at the bench to take a load off will look at your store—whether they intend to or not.
- *Pet-friendly image.* Convey a pet-friendly image. Provide a dog water fountain near your storefront. Pet lovers will love your store if they see that you also care for the well-being of their little darlings.
- *Cleanliness.* Always keep the sidewalk in front of your store in pristine condition. Avoid having leaves lie around in fall or snow in winter, and also pick up any trash left behind.

No matter where a store is located, sufficient parking facilities should always be provided. Sidney Kligmart of Sheldon Jewelry Co. said it all in a nutshell: "Our customers love the idea of parking in front of our store and walking directly in."[8] Usually, this technique won't work for shopping malls. Shoppers must often walk long distances to find the store. Therefore mall maps, as well as signage, should be provided at entrances to help customers find the way to different stores. In fact, research shows that parking lot characteristics considerably influence store choice.[9] Therefore, parking should be made as comfortable and as convenient as possible. Here's how:[10]

- *Special parking spaces.* Reserve parking spaces for special use (e.g., for maternity parking or expectant mothers). By going beyond what is required by law (parking for disabled shoppers), the store signals to their shoppers with special requirements that their needs are taken into full consideration.
- *Warning signage.* Warning signage used in a lot should communicate a benefit for customers whenever possible (e.g., "reserved parking—please keep this place free for expectant mothers").

- *Safety lighting*. To improve the real and perceived safety of customers, use adequate lighting in all areas of the lot. Again, it makes sense to communicate this benefit to customers: "For your safety, lights are provided on this parking lot."
- *Aisle markers*. Aisle markers and different-colored parking zones will help shoppers to remember where they have parked. Some lots also provide reminder tabs for parkers to take with them— another opportunity for store advertising and communication.

Signs Send the Message

Should a store's name be on the storefront? The answer to this question is not as obvious as it sounds. The Japanese fashion label Comme de Garçons does not use a store sign with its name at its New York–based store. You would never find this store, which enjoys great popularity among the fashion crowd and tourists alike, unless you know of its existence. Above an inconspicuous brick wall covered with graffiti, a hand-lettered sign next to a fire ladder indicates a car repair shop called Heavenly Body Works. Comme de Garçons chose this location based on the historical connection, geographical situation, and its atmosphere.[11] The store is located in West Chelsea, next to slaughterhouses and garages. Even if a shopper does find the store, it is not easy to enter. After walking through a metal tunnel, shoppers stand in front of a glass door. However, the door does not open as usual. Instead, the hand must reach through a hole in the door and cause the door to turn around on an invisible axis, so shoppers can slip through. Inside, the metal tunnel continues, so suddenly the shopper is standing in the middle of the store. Now the picture completely changes. Bright lights, white walls, and high ceilings now symbolize the exclusivity of the well-known fashion label.

The fashion store chain Abercrombie & Fitch uses a similar, albeit less radical, strategy in some of its stores. They increase the tension of shoppers by revealing absolutely no information on the storefront about what shoppers can expect to find inside. Brick or wooden facades ward off shoppers who do not belong to their primary target group (i.e., shoppers who are neither in their teens nor in their twenties).[12]

Why does this concept work? Both Comme de Garçons and Abercrombie & Fitch employ what is known as the "forbidden place" effect.

The store represents a secret room, a place that is secured like a private sanctuary. Not everyone is allowed to enter. However, when shoppers finally manage to overcome all the difficulties and gain entrance, they feel satisfied, relaxed, and are personally affirmed that they belong to the chosen group of unique shoppers who are allowed access to this unique place.[13]

Admittedly, this concept will not always work. Good signage is still one of the most effective and least costly methods of advertising a business.[14] Especially for retail or restaurant business, signs account for a considerable number of impulse visits. Indeed, one study claims that 46% of first-time customers of various businesses indicated they visited the store just because they saw the signs outside the store.[15] Nevertheless, a bad sign can still harm a business. Just think of neon signs that are missing a letter, producing quite interesting, but unintended, business names.[16] For example, when the "S" of the Scrapbook store in Littleton, Colorado, was broken, the sign mercilessly signaled to shoppers that the store sold, well, "crapbooks."

To prevent your business from such a dire fate, here is a short checklist of details to consider when choosing and using business signs:

- *Take local zoning regulations into account.* Especially if your store is located in a historic district, there will be specific requirements for the location of signs. Likewise, a shopping mall might have special provisions in place to ensure consistency of the mall's design.[17]
- *Make your sign easily recognizable.* Shoppers normally look at business signs for only a few seconds when walking or driving by. Make sure a sign is easy to read when driving by at 40 or 50 mph. Use appropriate-sized letters, and limit the sign to the store's name or its logo.[18]
- *Adjust your sign to the neighborhood.* If your store is located in a commercial area, inappropriate or particularly conspicuous signs can lead to sign competition between stores.[19] For example, if a shop puts up a 20-foot-tall sign, the shop next to it will put up a 25-foot-tall sign with blinking lights. The store opposite will try to attract even more attention by installing an 18-foot-tall waving chicken on the roof. By tacking certain

additional information on the signs, such as "credit cards accepted" or "$10 special," shoppers can easily get overstrained and feel overwhelmed. As so often is true in store design, less is more with signs as well. This truism is confirmed by an old joke: There are three, fiercely competitive hamburger joints on the same street. The first put up a large sign saying, "Best hamburgers in town!" Not to be outdone, the second displayed an even larger sign: "Best hamburgers in the country!" The third, however, rather modestly proclaimed, "Best hamburgers on this street."

- *Make your sign brand your business.* Since signs should reinforce your overall store image, they should look like the rest of the marketing communication tools you use (e.g., leaflets, business cards, and print ads). If you stay consistent with your sign communication, maybe one day your business will be as easily remembered for its signage as the golden arches of McDonald's are worldwide today.[20]
- *Make sure that signs are visible at all times by using appropriate lighting.* Signs advertise your business 24 hours a day, 365 days a year.[21] Therefore, they should be easily visible from a distance and illuminated as soon as twilight sets in.

A Window Wonderland Brings Customers Into the Store

Once attracted at the sidewalk, shopper attention will grow, and they will want to have a closer look at your store. This is exactly the right time to convince them that they do not want to miss visiting your store by using an appealing shopping window. Shopping windows have an incredible power to attract customers. Therefore, retailers will go to great lengths to create appealing shopping windows. A case in point is the Christmas window of the Irish department store Arnott. It included four villages, snow slopes, markets, and a zoo, with everything replicated in full forensic detail. In fact, more than 400 individual pieces were used to install the display, and more than 3,000 lights were used to illuminate the store front.[22]

Similar to signs, shopping windows have the potential to be one of the least costly and one of the most efficient marketing communication tools a business can use. Shopping windows tell shoppers what they will find inside the store. Additionally, store windows can tell customers how to use certain products and provide additional information. However, there are many things that won't work in store window design, such as inappropriate lighting, too many or too few items, inappropriate props, or outdated displays that aren't changed for a long time.[23]

To avoid these failures, a clear shopping window strategy is necessary. The crucial question is, what do you want to say with your shopping windows? Is your primary goal to convey a certain image? Or do you just want to get as many customers inside the store as possible? To maximize store traffic, display affordable mainstream merchandise in the window. If, on the other hand, conveying an exclusive store image is your primary goal, focus on innovative and upscale merchandise.[24] Unfortunately, it's hard to have your cake and eat it too. You have to choose.

Some general guidelines to consider for your shopping window design include the following:

- Tell shoppers through the window design precisely what is going on inside the store. For example, if you currently use the overall theme "summer feeling," use palm trees, sand, or a deck chair in the store window.[25]
- Change your windows at appropriate time intervals. As we know from the research on motivation, consumers have a thirst for variety. Once shoppers are attracted by a particular shopping window, it is much more difficult to attract them with the same design again in the future.
- Avoid empty storefronts. They do not produce a good image, even for a short period of time. While you are redecorating a shop window, install window posters that reflect the image of the overall store positively.[26]
- If possible, change a few things in the shopping window every day. Try promoting the product of the day, joke of the day, or special discount of the day. Another possibility is to place the store mascot every day in another place.[27] For example, a store selling winter sporting equipment could place a stuffed polar bear next to skis one day and on the next have the bear hidden behind ski boots, while all other things remain in the same position.

- Fantasy and imagination are good, but so is a healthy dose of realism. Use lifelike mannequins instead of unrealistic ones to help shoppers imagine how clothes will look on them.[28]
- Use a background wall in the window if you need additional space for the merchandise from the store. You can use this wall like any other wall in the store to present merchandise. Additionally, shoppers will not be as easily distracted, since the merchandise is presented in front of a neutral background.[29]
- If you don't need this additional space, just provide a good overview of everything in the store. By keeping the product displayed in a shop window just a few feet above ground and staggering the height of other fixtures in the store, a shopper will also see nearly everything located in the store.[30] Further, by providing pedestrians a clear sight into the store, security risks are reduced. In addition, many stores also will benefit from a natural light source.[31]
- Use affective or emotional stimuli as "hidden persuaders" (see Figure 3.4). For example, water features can act as eye-catchers in shopping windows. Similarly, signs of nature, such as plants or animals, will unconsciously attract shoppers.[32] Appropriate in-store graphics, such as smiling faces and happy people, evoke pleasant feelings (see chapter 5).

Figure 3.4. A shopping window that uses plants and faces as emotional stimuli.

Entering the Store

Impressed by a fascinating store window, the shopper eventually decides to visit the store. However, the necessity of making a good first impression doesn't end here. Although only a small piece of the overall picture, the design of the front door should not be ignored.[33] A well-designed store entrance will put visitors in the mood to buy. Here is what is necessary to do to make the entrance appealing:

- *Clearly indicate where to enter.* Some shoppers may find it difficult to find the entrance if it looks like the rest of the store front. Especially when huge shopping windows are used, the entrance must stand out starkly from the rest of the storefront.
- *Make the entrance free of barriers.* Avoid psychological, as well as physical, barriers. A store should not give shoppers any arguments against visiting the store. For example, a customer might experience a psychological barrier if the door offers no view into the store. Usually, shoppers will avoid entering a store if they do not know what they can expect inside. Unless you intend to consciously use the forbidden place principle we discussed earlier, show the first-time visitor clearly what to expect inside the store. Physical barriers can be stairs that hinder disabled persons, senior citizens, and shoppers with baby carriages. If the store is located above or below street level, use ramps instead of stairs to make your store fully accessible to all types of shoppers.
- *Welcome the shopper.* Shoppers should feel warmly welcomed from the first moment they enter the store. Signs that say, "Welcome, just come in and browse" or "Through these doors walk the nicest people in the world" will give shoppers a first positive impression of the inviting atmosphere inside your store. Similar messages can be used at the exit, saying, "Thank you for shopping with us" or "Have a safe trip home."[34]
- *Provide an overview of the store.* Once inside the store, let customers have an overview of the whole store right away. Instead of floor-to-ceiling racks, use presentation tables or low shelves positioned right after the entrance.[35]

If possible, you should have only one entrance to your store. Two or more entrances can lead to safety issues as well as a lack of control of customer flow. However, if a store does have two or more doors, every door should be considered a main entrance. In other words, one entrance should not be considered as less important or like a back door. By treating all entrances as equally important, shoppers will feel welcome no matter which door they choose to use to enter the store.

In general, there are three possibilities for designing a storefront (see Figure 3.5):

1. *Standard front.* The entrance is on the same level as the rest of the storefront. Usually, the entrance door is enclosed by shopping windows.

2. *Open front.* Stores in a shopping mall have the option of having no physical storefront. An open storefront entrance, however, has the same problems as a store with several entrances: There is less control of customer flow. Nevertheless, it has the advantage of attracting more customers because there is no door that can act as a psychological barrier.

3. *Recessed front.* To attract customers on a shopping street, a recessed front can be used. Shoppers will be able to have a detailed look at windows without being confronted with the traffic flow of pedestrians on the street. In addition, no congestion will occur if the door opens on a busy shopping street. Nevertheless, one must consider that more litter can blow into the entrance area. Consequently, care should be taken to clean this area regularly.[36]

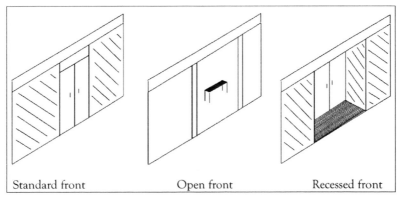

| Standard front | Open front | Recessed front |

Figure 3.5. Different types of store entrances.

The front door should convey the same clear message as the store windows. For example, if a seasonal sale is promoted in the windows, use similar decoration, such as posters, at the main entrance.

Interior Design: From the Floor to the Ceiling

Eventually, the shopper is in the store. In many stores, this is the perfect time for store clerks to offer the shopper a shopping basket or a cart. Usually, if shoppers are handed a shopping basket, it is quite unlikely that it will remain empty.[37] There are many store interior design factors that the shopper will encounter in the store, such as store fixtures and product displays. However, the first contact shoppers have with the store is usually with their feet.

Floor Covering

Touch, like the other senses, has an important influence on shopper buying behavior. Customers want to touch products or even shake a sales clerk's hand. However, usually little attention is paid to the material that every customer has contact with all the time. In a store, a shopper has the choice to decide whether to touch a product or not touch it. However, usually a shopper does not think where to place her next step.

Because touching the floor is something no shopper inside a store can avoid, wouldn't the floor be a great tool to use to influence shopping behavior? To find out, we conducted a study in a department store. The goal was to find out if the type of floor—hard or soft—influenced how fast shoppers walk. After all, as we had noticed during a beachside vacation far away from stores and shops, people tend to walk more slowly on soft sand. Was this just due to the relaxing vibes of that place, or was there more to it? Back home, we arranged for a soft carpet to be laid on top of the linoleum that usually covered one of the aisles in the store. These two types of floor were alternated on a daily basis while shoppers walking down the aisle were secretly observed. We found that shoppers walk considerably more slowly on a soft floor than on a hard one. They also tend to stop more frequently when stepping from one type of floor onto the next.[38]

This finding led us to advise retailers to vary floor coverings in a store or mall (see Figure 3.6). To increase the time that shoppers spend in certain areas of the store, a soft floor should be used (e.g., in the various merchandise presentations zones apart from the loop). Nevertheless, the loop leading customers through the store should not only be hard floors, as after all, we don't want to create a race track. In order to draw a shopper attention to as many products as possible, the stop rate can be increased by using different floor coverings. For example, if the general floor texture is linoleum, switching to a carpet at strategic locations can increase the likelihood that shoppers pause in front of products that retailers want emphasized, such as products with high profit margins. In contrast, there are areas in a store where shoppers should pass through at a faster pace (e.g., zones after the checkout area so as to avoid crowding). This is where a hard floor works well.

In general, the floor covering should match the overall store image:

- Wood floors will convey an exclusive image and ensure a more comfortable footing than will other nonresilient materials. Additionally, they absorb sounds. Unfortunately, they are expensive.

Figure 3.6. In this mall, a soft floor (carpet) is used in the front, and a hard floor (tile) in the back.

- Alternatively, if the store requires more resilient floors, asphalt, vinyl, or rubber tiles work. Usually, these types of materials are not used in the sale area, as they might convey a rather downscale image. Nevertheless, some store concepts allow the use of asphalt without it being perceived as inappropriate. Occasionally, furniture stores use asphalt in their self-service area, which is a combination of storage and sales areas. Rubber tiles are as durable as asphalt but do not look like road pavement; they also offer sound reduction. However, they are also expensive compared to the lower cost alternative, vinyl.

Finally, nonresilient materials like ceramic tiles, masonry, or terrazzo can be used. While ceramic tiles are a common floor covering in retailing due to their hard and durable characteristics, masonry and terrazzo are less popular, as they are quite expensive and also have specific requirements, such as floor resistance.

Materials: Either Just Another Brick in the Wall or a Wall's Creative Use

When shoppers try on shoes in the Timberland store in Freehold, New Jersey, they won't find it hard to imagine how their shoes will look and feel when wearing them in the great outdoors. A textural glass façade helps shoppers visually transport the outside environment to the inside of the store. Inside the store, only natural materials like bamboo, copper, and textured woods are used—all reinforce the natural image of the brand. Floors are made of bamboo; fixtures are made of reclaimed barn wood, metal, and glass. Shelves represent the brand image as well: They are made of environmentally friendly biofiberboard. The checkout counter is built of reclaimed wood with a stone top and decorated with an amber-tinted, seeded-glass backdrop. Stone is not just used for the checkout counter. The walls of the fitting room are also made of stacked stone in combination with frosted glass.[39]

Like many other successful stores, Timberland uses carefully chosen materials to convey its overall store image. This natural image addresses not only the shopper's visual sense but also their tactile sense to evoke emotions associated with nature. Research shows that most customers want to touch products before purchasing them.[40] Similarly, the texture of in-store fixtures and architectural elements can enhance a product's benefits. Shoppers tend to transfer associations evoked by materials used in a store to its products. An example is Timberland's use of wood, which is associated with nature.[41]

Timberland is not the only store that tries to recreate nature by using the right materials: Bayard, a ski and sportswear store located in Zermatt, Switzerland, also uses a lot of wood to convey the rustic and natural atmosphere associated with skiing and Swiss chalets (see Figure 3.7).

A store's materials should enhance its merchandise benefits and values. While plastic, with its presumed playful associations, represents an appropriate material in a toy store, it will negatively influence perceptions of quality in an electronics store. In the latter, metal (especially machined metal) can communicate to shoppers that the products there are durable and technologically superior.

Table 3.1 provides an overview of different materials used in stores and what consumers often associate with those materials.[42]

Figure 3.7. Wood is used in a ski store to convey the rustic and natural atmosphere associated with skiing and Swiss chalets.

Table 3.1. Materials Used in Store Design and Their Consumer Associations

Material	Associations for consumers
Brick	Durable, cozy, and natural
Glass	Fragile, modern, and fabricated
Wood	Natural and handmade
Iron and steel	Historical
Stainless steel	Aggressive and professional
Metals	Cold, sterile, and precise
Machined metal	Durable, robust, and technologically superior
Polymers	Bright, cheerful, and humorous
Ceramic	Rigid, cold, durable, hygienic, and long lasting
Plastic	Playful and low quality

Walls influence consumer behavior not only through the material used to build them but also through their shape. Straight walls, broken only by occasional sharp angles, evoke associations of masculinity, while curved walls elicit associations with femininity. In general, shoppers prefer shapes that represent their own body shape. Female shoppers will respond to curved walls more favorably than straight walls. Therefore, neutral products should be presented on a curved wall when targeting female shoppers and on a straight wall when addressing male shoppers. However, if the product is gender related (e.g., boxing gloves), consumers will respond to the product more favorably if the wall shape corresponds to the product's image, regardless of the shopper's gender.[43] Therefore, we advise presenting products associated with masculinity on straight walls and products associated with femininity on curved walls. If the product has no gender-related association, then the shape of the wall should be adjusted to the target gender group (e.g., curved walls for female shoppers; see Figure 3.8).

Displays: Unseen Often Stays Unsold

Shoppers often decide within a few seconds whether or not to take a closer look at merchandise. For this reason, information about products must be visible at first glance and be conveyed in the most efficient and

Figure 3.8. Curved walls used in a store that sells products to women.

easy manner. One option to capture shoppers' fickle attention is to use point-of-purchase (POP) displays.

A POP display is a flexible unit that is used to present merchandise. The unit can be a bin or a kiosk, but it does not necessarily need to be a tangible physical shelf. For example, in more than one supermarket, shelf stockers arranged soda cans so customers saw an oversized Super Mario figure.

POP displays can fulfill a number of functions:[44]

- *Create demand for specific products.* The first and foremost function of all displays is to create demand for particular products. According to industry statistics, in supermarkets, POP displays typically raise brand sales between 1.2 % and 19.6 %, depending on the product and display type. In drugstores, average brand sales increases via displays are somewhat lower at 6.5%.[45] POP displays containing innovative elements are particularly successful at capturing the attention of shoppers and consequently triggering unplanned purchases. Such innovative elements can be animated projections, electronic displays, electric clocks, or corrugated prepacks, to name just a few.[46]
- *Enhance the store image.* In line with the image of the store, dump bins where shoppers can root for bargains can be used,

or sophisticated displays can be used to promote exclusive merchandise.

- *Enhance shopping convenience.* Shoppers will find products more easily if the products are located on POP displays at the front of the store. Especially during promotions or special seasons (like Halloween), shoppers will appreciate finding the products they are seeking displayed near the entrance area.
- *Control in-store traffic movement.* POP displays can direct customer flow in a certain direction. For example, shopper attention can be directed to less frequently visited areas of the store by locating eye-catching POP displays in those sections.

A store that offers various brands (e.g., a supermarket) is faced with highly competing manufacturers who each want more shelf space or POP displays. However, too many or too many different POP displays will only confuse and overstrain shoppers. Therefore, retailers need to have very clear guidelines for how displays should look in order to convey a harmonious overall store picture and clearly communicate that to their suppliers.

Each display should contain four elements:

1. *Merchandise.* Which merchandise should be presented on the POP display? Depending on store type and overall store image, either products with the highest profit margin, latest arrival, newest reductions, or impulse purchase products can be promoted by POP displays.
2. *Props and color.* Props, such as mannequins and other accessories that show products in their usage context, as well as different colors, will support the effectiveness of POP displays. In general, strong colors like red or yellow will attract more attention than pastel colors will. Green displays, however, were found to make people hungry.[47]
3. *Lighting.* Ensure there is a special lighting source (e.g., a spot that is available and ready to put products in the right light).

4. *Show cards.* Use price tags if the POP display is used to promote special offers. Use benefit signs if the product is not price reduced but offers special benefits to shoppers.[48]

In general, there are two kinds of displays: content displays that provide shoppers with information (e.g., about the latest promotions) and product displays, which are mainly used for dual placement. A dual placement refers to a product's second location in the store, away from its regular placement in the shelf. For example, instant soups in a supermarket are often located in dump displays at the front of the store, offering special promotions such as "buy two, get one free." A shopper will find these same soups at their regular spot in the aisle that offers convenience foods.

Within these two categories, there are several kinds of possible displays (see Figure 3.9).

Content displays are used to communicate specific messages. They can either refer to a special promotion or be used to enhance the store's image. Based on their location in the store, there are various types of content displays (see Table 3.2).

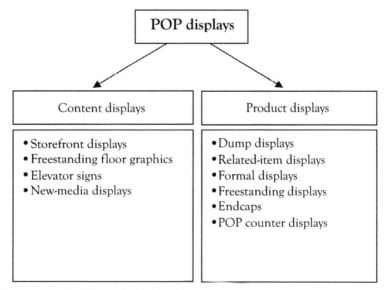

Figure 3.9. Different POP displays.

Table 3.2. Frequently Used Content Displays

Type of display	Characteristics
Storefront displays	• Located in the store window or in front of the store • Used to enhance a store's image • Use innovative displays for an up-to-date and state-of-the art image • **Examples:** A-board, wall-mounted flag, column stand, standing flag[49]
Freestanding floor graphics	• Display a specific content • Never compete with merchandise presented • Coordinate graphics and follow specific design guidelines[50] • **Examples:** Sign displays, poster frames
Elevator signs	• Display a specific content • Can be used to announce special events • **Examples:** Calendars to inform consumers about planned events and special promotions
New-media displays	• Use movement-activated images or touch-sensitive product displays • Provide central control of the actual point of sale • Increase customer involvement by providing touch screens • Enhance understanding of products by interactivity • Enhance customer comfort[51] • **Examples:** Digital touch screen stock checkers

Product supply displays are usually used to promote certain products, often in combination with price discounts. When deciding to use a product supply display, it is essential that display units are adaptable, interchangeable, and most importantly, accessible. A customer should be able to pull out the drawers, touch the goods, and carefully inspect them.[52] Table 3.3 offers an overview of various kinds of product supply displays.

Look Up and See the Ceiling

The Sistine Chapel in Rome has perhaps the most lauded ceiling in the world. However, there are many more ceilings worth discussing. When looking at the ceiling in the Bellagio hotel in Las Vegas, one immediately is immersed in a blaze of colors, consisting of thousands of hand-blown glass flowers. In Paris, tourists all over the world visit the Galleries Lafayette department store and see its unmistakable glass-domed ceiling (see Figure 3.10).[58]

Table 3.3. Product Supply Displays Often Used in Stores

Type of display	Characteristics
Dump displays	• Communicate a bargain image • Low maintenance • Easy to move[53] • Effective for low-cost and frequently purchased items[54] • **Example:** Bins filled with products such as accessories in an electronics store
Related-item displays	• Present numerous related items • Encourage sales, specifically unplanned or impulse purchases • **Example:** Snacks located next to beer
Formal displays	• Act as eye-catchers • Place at strategic points • Use "starter gaps" to suggest product is required[55] • **Example:** Product pyramids
Freestanding displays	• Located on aisles or near the front entrance to attract customers • Use for the latest or most exciting merchandise[56] • **Examples:** Mannequins or fixtures
End caps	• Are flexible shelving units located at the end of aisles • Increase unplanned or impulse purchases • Perfectly suited to display merchandise with high margins. • Used alone or consecutively to create rows as in drug stores[57] • **Example:** An endcap used to display snacks at the end of the soft drink aisle
POP counter displays	• Located near the checkout counter • Also called multi-item displays • **Example:** Display unit used for items like gum, candy, batteries, and magazines

Indeed, a ceiling can enhance the overall image of a store. Beside the cost, three factors must be considered when deciding which ceiling to use:

1. *Performance.* This aspect refers to visual aesthetics, acoustical performance, light reflection, and durability. Using an appealing ceiling will create, define, and enhance a store's brand identify. Depending on the store, different levels of noise absorption are required. A noise-intensive retail store will provide a popular image; however, more exclusive stores might appreciate ceiling panels that reflect sounds to enable conversations between customers and the sales

Figure 3.10. The domed ceiling at the Galleries Lafayette makes this department store stand out from the competition.

staff. Light-reflecting materials enable illumination of the whole store at a low cost. Finally, ceilings should be chosen based on their durability to ensure there is a long-lasting, beautiful design.[59]

2. *Design.* In combination with store fixtures, lighting, and walls, varying ceiling heights or designs can draw shopper attention to specific areas of a store.[60]

3. *Ceiling height.* In rooms with high ceilings, individuals feel better and sense a higher energy level than in rooms with low ceilings. This was found in in-store experiments where consumers had more ideas on how to use a product (in addition to its conventional use) when it was presented in a room with a high ceiling.[61] Additionally, in rooms with high ceilings, shoppers evaluate products holistically

without paying close attention to their details. This response can be used by chain stores that thrive on high volume. In contrast, to convince shoppers to inspect a product in detail (e.g., in jewelry stores), lower ceiling heights are often used because a lower ceiling makes shoppers focus more on the specifics of the products.[62]

Mirrors: Losing Weight at a Glance

Several fashion stores use the trick of flattering mirrors. These add inches to a shopper's height and shave pounds from the hips. Flattering mirrors are created with the right combination of a thin piece of glass (thicker glass will make people look green), natural light projected from the front to soften unflattering shadows, and warm wall colors in the fitting room. The mirror should be full length and slightly inclined away from the viewer.[63] Naturally, shoppers who are flattered by their own image in these mirrors are more likely to buy. However, at the same time, more of these shoppers will bring fashion items back to the store after they try them on again at home.[64]

Mirrors can be used not only to make shoppers slimmer but also to visually enlarge a store. For the same reason, mirrors are located in elevators to reduce the risk of claustrophobia. If space is limited, locating mirrors on both sides of a shop will enhance the perceived size of the store.[65] However, it makes a difference whether mirrors are placed vertically or horizontally. If a vertical mirror is used, shoppers will see themselves making "yes" movements with their heads when looking up and down, while the opposite holds for horizontal mirrors—that is, "no" movements. Indeed, this behavior has been found to have important implications on product assessment. Products in stores with vertical mirrors get more positive assessments. In addition, customers appear to be more likely to approach or consider the store goods in a positive manner and thus end up purchasing more goods.[66]

Checkout Counters

We are almost at the end of this chapter, so it's time to pay for purchases. When designing your store, you should pay a lot of attention to the design of your checkout counter. Here are just a few questions to ponder:

- How many checkout stations or checkout counters will you provide?
- How much space do you need to consider for waiting lines?
- How can you keep your customers happy during waiting time?

The influence of long waiting lines should not be underestimated. Indeed, making people wait can cost a store sales. Customers tend to evaluate the store atmosphere negatively when they expect that they will have to wait in the store.[67] Since long waiting lines can scare off customers, decisions relating to the store's waiting-line system should be well reasoned and organized. Of course, the question referring to the number of checkout stations depends also on the store you intend to open. You will need more checkout stations for a supermarket than you will for a specialty store. Additionally, the question of how much space you have to allocate for your cash register area goes hand in hand with the question of how you manage these lines.

One cash line configuration that more and more stores are implementing is to have one single checkout line, divided into several cash registers at the end. Admittedly, the line will get much longer compared to having separate lines for each cash register. Nevertheless, when Whole Foods in Manhattan began using the single-line system, the store became immediately well known as the supermarket with the fastest grocery store lines.[68] If you decide to use the conventional system with several lines, you can also communicate that you will open more cash registers if a predefined number of customers are waiting in the line.

Another way to keep perceived waiting time as short as possible is to distract customers during wait time. This can be easily achieved by drawing the attention of customers to frequently bought products nearby. For example, supermarkets offer candy, razors, and magazines at the checkout counter.[69] Similarly, large electronic stores place accessories in baskets in the waiting area where people can kill time rummaging around for USB cables, computer mice, mouse pads, or laser pointers. In fact, placing merchandise near the cash register not only turns customer attention away from a (long) waiting line but also increases impulse purchases. However, there are several other possibilities you must consider to make the checkout as comfortable as possible:

- *Ten-items-or-less lines.* Fast checkout lines will increase the convenience of a shopping trip and also let shoppers buying only a few items get faster service.
- *Self-scanning checkouts.* Shoppers appreciate a fast alternative even though they have more than 10 or 15 items. Research has found that control, reliability, ease of use, and enjoyment are important factors that lead customers to use self-scanning options. However, self-scanning should not entirely replace service checkouts totally because the same study also showed that some shoppers think that they have the right to be served[70] or simply don't feel comfortable with self-checkout technology.
- *No-candy checkouts.* Although some shoppers appreciate buying candy during waiting time, for families with little children, sweets at the checkout counter can make shopping very stressful. In order to keep little children from grabbing candy and exhausting mother's nerves, provide one or two lines with, for instance, batteries or other snacks, such as granola bars, instead of candy.
- *Stress-reducing atmosphere.* The atmosphere can decrease perceived waiting time. For example, green or blue colors can evoke calm and relaxed feelings in the waiting line.

In the end, a friendly cashier will do the rest and be the one to convince a shopper that it was worth waiting to buy his selections.

Takeaway Points

Here are the most important takeaway points from this chapter:

- Successful store design starts with the right location.
- In a mall, a store should be located next to stores that target the same audience or near food venues. Avoid locations in transition zones. Shoppers will focus on the changing environment and not on your store.
- Use store design techniques to make parking as comfortable and as convenient as possible for shoppers.
- Use the floor to influence shoppers' walking behavior: Soft floor coverings will slow shopper walking speed.

- Adjust the materials in the store to the merchandise. Do not use too many different materials to try to convey a harmonious store image.
- Shoppers have specific associations with the materials used in a store. Consequently, materials should be used that enhance the store's benefits and values.
- Two kinds of displays are used in stores. Content displays provide shoppers with information (e.g., about promotions). Product supply displays are mainly used for dual placement to encourage spontaneous purchases.
- Use only a limited number of POP displays, or aisles will quickly look cluttered.
- The checkout area is your last chance to make a good impression on shoppers before they leave the store. Keep the perceived waiting time as short as possible (e.g., by using only one waiting line ending in several checkout counters).

CHAPTER 4

Visual Merchandising

Capturing Customer Attention

On a lovely Saturday morning, John and Erica are walking along a street when suddenly their attention is caught by a farmers' market. They hear the loud and confident calls of market vendors offering fresh vegetables and other delicious-looking food. They decide to go and look more closely at the market stands. They are immediately fascinated by a produce stand featuring artistic pyramids of various fresh produce. Some fruits with similar colors are placed close to each other and give the stand a harmonious overall appearance. The couple notices a cornucopia of exotic fruits, including a stack of coconuts that are positioned next to a picture showing a pristine, palm-studded beach. John and Erica are simply not able to resist the temptation, and before moving on, they buy a large amount of fruit, some of which they have never tasted before. Welcome to the world of visual merchandising.

What Is Visual Merchandising?

In a nutshell, visual merchandising is the art and science of presenting products in the most visually appealing way. Visual merchandising is the "language of a store"—it is how a retailer communicates with its customers through product images or presentations. Just as every language has its own grammar and logic, visual merchandising has its own rules and principles, too. We explore them in this chapter.

Although visual merchandising is frequently associated with apparel retailing, there are many ways to present many kinds of products to their best advantage. For example, to present clothes in the most appealing way, elegant mannequins are often used, whereas a bakery might present their most refined cupcakes on a beautifully crafted silver tray. Vegetables in a supermarket can be arranged according to color, and a perfumery can use eye-catching presentation tables to display its products visually (see Figure 4.1).

With a good visual merchandising strategy, products will almost sell themselves. In fact, a study examining the effect of visual merchandising for consumer packaged goods found that the impact of merchandising support on brand switching was approximately equal to a 15%–30% price cut.[1] A more sophisticated visual merchandising strategy can lead to even greater effects, achieved by directing shoppers' attention to specific products, triggering unplanned purchases, and establishing a uniform picture of the store.

In addition, the presentation of merchandise will contribute to the overall image of the store. For instance, a discount retailer might use simple pallets for visual merchandise presentation, whereas a specialty grocery store could use smart display tables, shelves, and cabinets with products displayed artistically. Therefore, it is very important that the correct visual merchandise strategy combines with all other elements of the store design, such as the store layout or the store atmosphere, to convey a harmonious overall store image.

When planning visual merchandising, several aspects must be considered. As so often happens in marketing, it helps to look at visual

Figure 4.1. Visual merchandising in a perfumery.

merchandising from the customer's perspective. What do customers expect from the product presentation when they enter a store? A shopper's needs that are supposed to be fulfilled by a store can be summarized by three principles.[2]

Make Merchandise Visible

Although this point seems to be obvious, this was not what we found in some of the stores we visited and analyzed over 20 years. Sometimes we found merchandise was hidden behind large point-of-purchase (POP) displays. This may be great for the merchandise on display, but we strongly feel that the products in less prominent positions have a right to be seen as well. On other occasions, the products were missing from store shelves completely. They were simply not regularly restocked, and no effort was made to conceal the gaps. Half-empty shelves may have been the norm in the Eastern Bloc prior to the revolution in the late 1980s, but they are inexcusable in the current age of inventory control systems. However, shoppers will only buy what they see. Therefore, it is the essential task of visual merchandising to make products visible.

Make Merchandise Tangible and Easily Accessible

Shoppers tend to touch most products before buying them. While eyesight is the most dominant sense through which humans gather information, touching helps shoppers make an emotional connection with a product. Seeing is believing, but touching is feeling. The softness of that cashmere sweater, the steady and secure grip of a cell phone, the sensuous curves of a shampoo bottle, and the feeling of sitting on a soft sofa— they all sell the product. Furthermore, giving the shopper a chance to feel products is a major advantage that brick-and-mortar stores have over online retailers.

Nevertheless, many retail stores often use locked display cases or find other ways to prevent customers from helping themselves and selecting the products (e.g., placing them on high shelves that petite shoppers have no chance of reaching). While it is understandable to keep expensive jewelry under lock and key to prevent shoplifting, is it really necessary to keep condoms in locked glass displays, as is it simply standard traditional practice in many drugstores? How many paramours who are too timid to ask a salesclerk to unlock the display case have turned away over the years, frustrated and dissatisfied with that store?

Another customer group that wants fast and easy access to their desire is booklovers. Recently we visited a dazzling Japanese bookstore in Bangkok, Thailand. The store looked great from a macro perspective. When we took a closer look at the books, however, we were shocked. Every single one of the thousands of books in this tore was individually wrapped in an impenetrable plastic wrapper. A sign on each bookshelf declared, "Kindly unwrap the book at the nearest counter." We did that with the first two books, but then we stopped. After all, how many books can you expect a kindly smiling salesclerk to unwrap for you? This was one of the very few occasions that we left a bookstore without making a purchase.

For many products, shoppers do not want to see just the packaging, but the product as well. Therefore, stores where such products are sold should display a selection of unpacked goods. For example, an electronic store should have a selection of demonstration cameras on display to allow the customer to feel each product, see how it works, and decide whether to purchase it based on their own experience. Many demonstration products may, of course be, unusable after having been touched by thousands of shoppers, but isn't that a small price to pay for the many additional products sold?

Give Shoppers Good Choices

Consumers want to have full control of what they are doing. Visual merchandising should be used to give consumers a feeling of freedom of choice, not that they are being forced into making a purchase. Some stores offer only relatively few choices on purpose. This strategy follows the scarcity principle. The scarcity principle is based on the assumption that because valuable objects are rare, artificially limiting their range or availability will increase the perceived value of those goods.[3] Examples are limited editions or sales items that are available for only a very short period of time. The scarcity principle can be part of a successful visual merchandising strategy. If it is used excessively, however, it can restrain a shopper's perceived freedom, which will in turn lower the shopping enjoyment. At the same time, there is also a dark side to having choices.

If shoppers are confronted with too many products, they get overloaded. Therefore, measures have to be taken to reduce the risk of overstraining customers and provide a balanced display of choices that works for the customer. We will come back to this point in the next section.

Less Is More: A Key Principle of Good Product Presentation

Imagine you are in a supermarket where a wide variety of different types of jam are for sale. You see strawberry, blackberry, grape, raspberry, apple, peach, gooseberry, red currant, black currant, cranberry, kiwi, and many more. You name it, and they have it. All in all, there are 24 different flavors. Now let's change the scenery. In this new scenario, the supermarket sells only the 6 most popular flavors. Would you rather buy a jar of jam where 24 flavors are offered or where you can choose from only 6?

When asked this question, many consumers had no difficulty answering. Their gut feeling tells them, "Choice is good for you!" Consequently, they state that they would prefer to have a choice of many flavors of jam instead of just a few. After all, isn't choice a fundamental value in American society? Over time, the number of products consumers can choose from has thus increased dramatically. In 1949, a typical supermarket carried 3,750 different products. Today, it offers approximately 45,000 items.[4] Choice may be good in general, but when faced with a huge variety of products in a store, the situation can become somewhat different.

The two scenarios we described were part of an in-store experiment conducted by two psychologists, Sheena Iyengar and Mark Lepper. In an upscale supermarket in California, shoppers encountered a tasting booth with either 24 or 6 different flavors of jam. Considerably more shoppers (60%) were attracted to the booth offering an extensive selection of flavors as opposed to the booth with the limited selection (only 40%). The results were drastically different, however, when sales were measured. Of all shoppers who had tasted a jam from the limited selection, 30% made a purchase, but only a meager 3% who had experienced the large selection bought a jar of jam.[5]

In light of these findings, it seems that having many choices does not necessarily benefit consumers or their choices. Several studies have already examined this phenomenon, also called "the tyranny of choice," revealing the clear negative consequences of too much choice. Shoppers making a choice from too many options regret their purchase decision afterward much more than do shoppers choosing from a limited choice set. Additionally, as shoppers are overwhelmed, they decide not to make any choice at all. As a result, they leave the store without purchasing any of the alternatives, either because they have decided to postpone the decision to a later point in time or—in the worst case—because they gave up on making any purchase at all. By optimizing the visual merchandising strategy of a store, these undesirable consequences can be avoided. There are two solutions:

1. *Reduce the number of items carried in the store.* Many stores have successfully reduced the number of stock keeping units (SKUs) for sale. One of them is Trader Joe's supermarkets. This highly successful grocery chain, concentrated primarily in California but now expanding all over the United States, carries only 4,000 items: less than one-tenth the number carried by a typical supermarket.[6] Each of the products it sells, though, is carefully selected to ensure that it is of the highest quality.

2. *Structure the assortment of products.* Offering only a limited selection of merchandise may be helpful to ease the burden shoppers have in deciding which products to choose. However, the jam experiment also showed that shoppers are more attracted to a large selection than to a small one. To have the best of both worlds, here is what we have found to work for many retailers: Arrange products clearly and selectively. This effect can be achieved by emphasizing only a few alternatives but also by having the other alternatives available if requested. For example, record stores often feature the top ten records of the week.

Similarly we rearranged the assortment of a wine store. Instead of giving equal emphasis to all the wines, we preselected several wines in each section of the store. With this new arrangement, wine lovers were still impressed by the vast assortment of wines our client's store is famous for. At the same time, shoppers also saw recommended wines in each of the sections: five recommended champagnes, five recommended dessert wines, and so on. The preselected wines were visually emphasized in a straight and simple way by putting them on little pedestals on each shelf and adding a sign that stated, "Recommended—our customers' favorite wines." While the true wine experts continued to make their own, very personal selections, the vast majority of shoppers now had a much easier way of choosing—which ultimately was reflected in higher sales (see Figure 4.2).

There Are Different Ways to Present Your Merchandise

It is Sunday morning, and Steve decided to do something that he should have done a long time ago—buy a new dining table. He had postponed this purchase as long as possible, but with one side of the table standing on boxes instead of on a table leg, it was high time to get a new table. Steve thinks back with horror on his last trip to the furniture store, where he was confronted with an overwhelming number of sideboards closely pitched in a row. The purchase decision took 2 hours, and in the end the sideboard he chose turned out to be too bulky for his small studio apartment. Anyway, he overcame his inhibitions this time and drove to the store. He entered the store reluctantly, expecting to see more confusingly arranged products. However, he recognizes with the first step that the store has changed. Instead of presenting dinner tables in one corner,

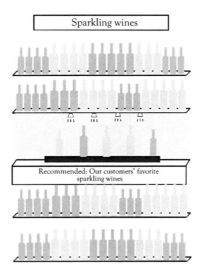

Figure 4.2. Clearly arranged product presentation showing a few highlighted products.

couches in another corner, and kitchens on the second floor, a wide aisle leads shoppers from one fully equipped room to another, separated by thin walls. Steve follows the aisle and enters a room exactly the same size as his apartment. The room looks nearly as comfortable as his own apartment, with beautifully arranged pillows on the couch, bookcases, and an attractive small dining table. It doesn't take long before Steve is convinced that this table will look at least as good in his apartment. As he enjoyed the chairs as well as the tableware, he spontaneously decides to buy four chairs and new tableware as well. Steve had just been exposed to what retail experts call a "bundled presentation."

Bundled presentations are just one of the methods stores can use to present merchandise. In this section, we want to give a short overview of the aims of merchandise presentations, followed by a discussion of the different methods used to present merchandise—including Steve's favorite, the bundled presentation.

In general, merchandise presentations aim at providing a clearly understandable picture of the whole store. In the end, shoppers should easily find what they are looking for. Naturally, the arrangement of an assortment depends on the products offered. For example, an apparel store will arrange products according to its brands, styles, or sizes. In contrast, a grocery store has to consider additional product characteristics, such as expiration date or weight. Nevertheless, there are some points to consider, irrespective of which products are offered:[7]

- *Present merchandise in an easily understandable way.* For example, present products in a logical sequence (e.g., tops and jackets on the upper half of a wall, skirts and trousers on the lower half; sizes should be arranged in ascending order).
- *Facilitate the decision process by merchandise presentation.* Products should be not only clearly arranged within their category but also presented to suggest additional items to shoppers. For example, in a grocery store, mixtures of spices could be located next to the meat corner. Shoppers will appreciate being reminded of products they might have forgotten to purchase—and this won't hurt sales.
- *Locate products at an appropriate height.* Whenever possible, do not place products too high (customers do not want to look

up) or too low (customers do not want to bend down or kneel; see chapter 1).

- *Try to avoid gaps.* Immediately refill shelves if an item sells out. For example, you can use shelves with automatic feeding, which are often used for items such as cans of drinks.

With all these suggestions in mind, a visual merchandising strategy can be easily developed. Whether a store looks appealing or not, however, depends to a large extent on the use of props, mannequins, and displays.

Props, Mannequins, and Displays: Use Them Effectively

Props refer to something used to clarify the function of the merchandise being sold or to tell a story about that merchandise. Props are usually not for sale, such as plastic food models used in the fruit section of a supermarket or a dressed mannequin. A do-it-yourself (DIY) store can present a lawnmower on Astroturf (an artificial lawn) with watering cans and some plastic flowers on it.

Props represent important tools used to achieve one main aim of visual merchandising: attracting customers even over a long distance. If they are sufficiently surprising and arousing, pedestrians will cross the street to have a more detailed look at the merchandise presented in a shopping window. Similarly, props can also be used to attract customer attention in the store. To enhance the effectiveness of props, apply the following rules:

- *Use the appropriate amount of merchandise.* If too few items are presented on or near a prop, it will seem that the product is sold out or, worse still, that the store is going out of business. In contrast, when using a prop with too many items, the selling message will get lost, and the store will appear aesthetically offensive to the shopper.[8] For example, if the DIY store presents three lawnmowers instead of only one, the shopper might not even notice the Astroturf and flowers used to support or accessorize the presentation.
- *Display appropriate accessories near the prop.* A bakery can sell packs of fine sugar—displayed in a crystal bowl—with cookies,

so customers can sprinkle the cookies with sugar at home to make them look nice. In the apparel industry, you can present necklaces, bags, or tights next to a mannequin.

- *Locate the displayed product near the prop.* There are few things that annoy customers more than being unable to find what they are looking for. If a customer wants to purchase a product seen on a display, you must make sure that she will immediately find this product in the desired size and the desired color nearby.

- *Change the props at regular intervals.* How often a prop has to be changed depends on the season and the change of the overall store theme. However, as a general rule, no prop should remain until it collects dust.[9] If you use mannequins, fittings should be always done in a noncustomer zone.[10] Some customers might have unpleasant feelings when they watch a mannequin's arm being dislocated to dress her.

- *Display mannequins from a three-fourths perspective.* Instead of positioning mannequins so consumers will see them from the front, you should turn them so that the first thing that catches the customer's eye is the mannequin from a three-fourths perspective (see Figure 4.3).[11]

Figure 4.3. Showing mannequins at a three-fourths perspective.

Props and mannequins can be used with every product presentation method. In general, two different presentation methods are used: traditional arrangement and bundled presentations.

The Traditional Presentation Method

Conventional presentation methods group products by their taxonomic category (e.g., different kinds of tables, such as couch tables, dining tables, desks) or by their status (luxury goods vs. everyday products). For example, in electronic stores, TV sets are often arranged by size. Another grouping possibility would be to place all TV sets by the same manufacturer side by side. In other words, all products in their various forms (e.g., different brands, different sizes) are located next to each other.

There are several possibilities for using props in a traditional merchandise presentation. For example, you can place a barrel in the wine division of a supermarket. In Figure 4.4 the barrel alludes to the traditional ripening of wine, and the touch screen to the left can be used by customers to get more information—an interesting and charming contrast.

Colors in combination with lighting effects can also be used to make your product presentation more appealing. For example, in a grocery store, blue light could be used in the fish section and red light in the meat section. Fruits

Figure 4.4. Traditional presentation with props.

can be presented in baskets made of natural materials. Nevertheless, you must ensure that the props do not outshine the promoted product. For example, if a small packet of sun block is displayed on a heap of sand with a deck chair, palms, and towels on it, the attention of the shopper will be drawn to the props and not the product simply because size attracts attention.

Bundled Presentations

More and more purchase decisions are made at the actual point of sale. On average, over one-third of purchase decisions in department stores are made on impulse.[12] In fact, in some categories, spontaneous purchases make up to 80% of all purchases.[13] Because many shoppers decide on their purchases right in the store, a good visual merchandising strategy can boost spontaneous purchases. One way to achieve this is by the use of bundled presentations.[14] In a bundled presentation of related products (i.e., products that are often used together), the products are presented in close proximity to each other. An example of such a bundled presentation is shown in Figure 4.5. Instead of presenting bread on one shelf, wine on another shelf, and baskets on yet another shelf (the left side of Figure 4.5) in a bundled presentation, these products would be presented in a picnic basket (the right side of Figure 4.5). In order to capture the full potential of a bundled presentation, it is not enough to only display related products. Props such as a meadow and a tree are used to reinforce the usage context and inspire the shopper's fantasy about using the product.

There are different ways to select the products to present in a bundled presentation:

Figure 4.5. Traditional presentation (left) and bundled presentation (right).

- *Usage context.* Products often used together because they supplement each other in usage can be combined in a bundled presentation. For example, in a furniture store, tables, chairs, and tableware can be presented next to each other (see Figure 4.6).
- *Occasions.* Products can be grouped according to their use for particular occasions. For example, around Halloween, a supermarket could present pumpkins, as well as candy, on artfully decorated displays.
- *Fantasy theme.* Products associated with a common theme can be presented together. For instance, a stationer could present products for school children along with a fitting movie or television theme like *Star Wars*, *Lord of the Rings*, or the activities of a star like Hannah Montana.

The biggest advantage of bundled presentations is that shoppers get a better idea of how products can be used and which products complement one another well. This knowledge leads to desirable consequences for retailers. Shoppers in a store that employs bundled presentations evaluate the products considerably better compared to shoppers in a store

Figure 4.6. Bundled presentation (complementary relationship) for a dining area.

that only displays merchandise in a traditional way. In addition, bundled presentations have even been shown to put shoppers in a better mood.[15]

In most stores, shoppers don't remove a product they like directly from the bundled presentation. If they did, the sales staff would have to redecorate the dining table you saw in Figure 4.6 on a daily, perhaps even hourly, basis. Instead, retailers usually keep the products that are for sale on store fixtures that are away from the bundled presentation. This made us wonder if a bundled presentation still has a positive effect on the shopper once the shopper has left the bundled presentation vicinity and sees the product naked, without other complementary products and props.

To address this question, we conducted an experiment in a furniture store. Shoppers had to evaluate a couch that was presented either as part of a living room (Figure 4.7) or in a traditional presentation where the couch was located next to other couches. The results indicate that a bundled presentation improved the shoppers' evaluation of the product even when the product was first displayed in a bundled presentation and only afterward evaluated in a traditional product display.[16] These results are good news for retailers because they show that a bundled presentation lingers in the mind of shoppers even when shoppers do see the product again on a shelf.

Figure 4.7. Bundled presentation showing a couch as part of a living room.

Planograms

With all this strategic merchandising advice and discussion in mind, it is often difficult to put all the tools and techniques into actual practice. Therefore, we advise using planograms to plan and communicate to the store personnel where and how merchandise should be located.

A planogram is a schematic drawing of shelves or another type of store fixture that helps to make optimal use of available shelf space in a retail store.[17] Planograms are a useful tool to use to facilitate a clear arrangement of your merchandise. A planogram used in a fashion store could look like Figure 4.8.

Planograms are not just used in fashion retailing; they can be used in all types of stores. The complexity of a planogram can vary, ranging from an exact photograph of a shelf arranged particularly for this purpose to a sketch or even a computer-based visualization. Planograms fulfill several important functions:

- Facilitate product replenishment.
- Create a uniform picture for a branch chain.
- Enable planning product allocation in advance.

In addition, a planogram enables sales staff to keep a record of the number of items displayed in conjunction with the store's inventory systems. Planograms help avoid out-of-stock problems.

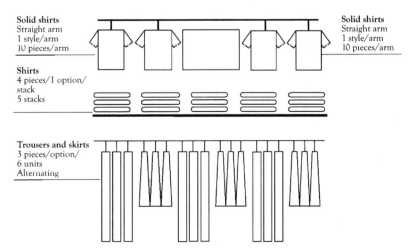

Figure 4.8. Use of a planogram in a fashion store.

Using Magnets: Draw Attention to Products via Intensity, Contrast, and Position

The intensity of a stimulus represents one means of creating attention.[18] All stimuli addressing the human senses can be varied according to the intensity desired. For example, a large feature wall will attract more attention than a small one. Likewise, brighter areas of a store will get more attention than darker areas. Louder music will attract more attention than soothing music. Intense colors (e.g., red) will highlight products more than less intense colors (e.g., pastel shades). All these properties can be used effectively to draw a shopper's attention to merchandise. For example, a feature wall showing one type of product, but in different kinds or colors, will act as an eye-catcher in the store (see Figure 4.9).

Contrasting stimuli, also referred to as collative stimuli, will also attract shopper attention. Collative stimuli are either surprising, new, or unusual. They increase people's attention because they cause a change in the sensory system.[19] For example, building a huge pyramid showing apparel merchandise will get the attention of customers, as it is an unusual presentation method.[20] Likewise, a rearrangement of merchandise attracts interest due to its novelty. Nevertheless, too much novelty in a store will result in consumer confusion and

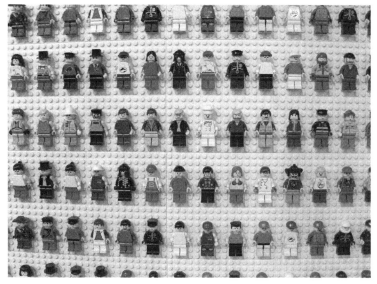

Figure 4.9. Use intensity to create attention.

overwhelm shoppers. Therefore, new and traditional stimuli should always be kept balanced. For example, when merchandise in the entrance area is replaced by new arrivals, the rest of the merchandise should keep their prior placement. In other words, do not change everything at the same time.

Finally, position is another way to catch shopper attention. Simply put, if you place a product in a spot where most shoppers look, it will get noticed. As discussed in chapter 1, this effect can be achieved by presenting products that should get noticed at the appropriate height on a shelf as well as in areas of the store that receive the most store traffic.

Tap Into Shopper Emotions With In-Store Graphics

We have already discussed the strong influence that emotions can have on shopping behavior. However, emotions can be influenced not only by atmospheric factors, such as scents, music, or colors, but also by in-store graphics, a popular visual merchandising tool. Some pictures simply contribute to a more pleasant shopping experience. That concept by itself is already a positive thing. Some pictures, however, are special. They tap deep into the shopper's psyche and invoke schemas—networks of related associations in the mind of the consumer—for those specific emotional experiences shared by a large number of people. There are three types of schema-invoking pictures, which differ in the way in which they have an effect, ranging from universal to local:[21]

1. *Archetypes and pictures leading to biologically programmed reactions* will have an effect on the largest number of shoppers, as their effect is independent of individual experiences. Because they are deeply rooted in the human mind, they can be expected to lead to particularly strong emotional experiences. Archetypes are images that often appear in stories and myths. Examples are the hero, the wise old man or woman, the temptress, the regular guy, and the outlaw, to name just a few. Archetypes that can be translated into pictures can also relate to nature (e.g., a remote, snow-covered summit) or even stories, such as *The Quest* or *Rags to Riches*.[22] An even stronger emotional reaction can be achieved by pictures that trigger biologically programmed reactions (see Figure 4.10). An example is the baby schema: It is evoked by a set of features possessed by babies, namely, big eyes, a large, round face, and full lips. Such pictures immediately capture our attention. This is nature's way

Figure 4.10. Pictures that trigger biologically programmed reactions can lead to strong emotional experiences.

to make sure that babies receive the attention and nurture they need to prosper. The baby schema is perceived as cute and communicates a feeling of warmth and comfort. It doesn't even matter all that much if the big eyes and round face belong to a human baby or a pet.

2. *Pictures evoking culture-specific schemas* have the second strongest effect. They trigger emotional schemas in shoppers of the same cultural background. For example, to put American shoppers in a vacation mood, pictures associated with the Tropics (e.g., palm trees, beaches, the ocean) can be displayed in a store.

3. *Target group–specific pictures* will primarily evoke emotions of a specific group of shoppers. An example of such an image would be a picture of football players midplay, which will have an emotional effect on football fans.

Examples of schema-invoking in-store graphics can be found in Figures 4.11, 4.12, and 4.13. Figure 4.11 shows how an archetypal in-store graphic of a rose can invoke a romance schema in the fine-china section of a housewares store. Figure 4.12 is an example of the Tropics schema, and Figure 4.13 is an example of a target group–specific picture intended to invoke the schema of a successful businessman.

Figure 4.11. A picture of a rose can activate a romance schema.

Figure 4.12. This picture can activate a Tropics schema.

Figure 4.13. A target group–specific picture invoking the "successful businessman" schema.

Emotional pictures will not only evoke specific emotions in the store but also act as eye-catchers and attract shoppers. One study commissioned by a department store found that large in-store graphics considerably increased patronage intentions. Twice as many customers visited the store when the in-store graphic was used. In addition, the store recorded an increase in sales of 17%. Motion pictures projected on the wall by a video projector yielded an even more impressive result. Store traffic rose by 116% and produced additional sales of 20%.[23] While these results may not be as impressive in every type of store, the study does reinforce the potential of inducing specific emotional experiences in shoppers through the use of in-store graphics.

Workable Aesthetics: Beauty Is Not Just in the Eye of the Beholder

Never underestimate the effects of beauty. Did you know that shoppers have a tendency to consider sales clerks more competent, knowledgeable, and likeable when the clerks are attractive? This view seems somewhat superficial and unfair, doesn't it? But it is what we found in a recent study.[24] What's more, even the merchandise is evaluated better when sold by an attractive salesperson. The focus of this book is, however, not on the sales staff, but on the store environment. The sales staff is a topic for another book.

Instead, we want to provide you here with ideas for how to make your merchandise presentation more attractive. In line with the psychology of perception, certain basic principles will help you make your product displays more aesthetically pleasing to gain a competitive advantage. But first we have to ask a key question: What is beauty? As one well-known saying states, "Beauty is in the eye of the beholder." Of course, there is truth in that. However, there are certain general features that are universally considered beautiful.[25] These are described next.

Unity: Convey a Harmonious Picture

Unity refers to the physical appearance of elements that are perceived as belonging together.[26] It is an important visual merchandising principle.

From the very first moment that shoppers enter a store, they will try to comprehend that store as a unified whole. A harmonious picture will facilitate that process. In general, human beings perceive elements that visually belong together as beautiful. Therefore, a visual merchandising strategy should follow corporate design guidelines. These guidelines include the use of colors, props, or general presentation methods. For example, a supermarket should try to arrange equally sized products next to each other. Indeed, a shelf showing products of the same size will be perceived as more beautiful than a shelf holding many different product sizes. There is symmetry here—that is, unity and harmony of image.

Balance: Create a Harmonious State of Equilibrium

There are two kinds of balance. The first type refers to an individual's specific expectations.[27] Even before shoppers enter a store, they have expectations about what they will see. If these expectations are not fulfilled, the store will not be perceived as balanced. Therefore, the presentation of merchandise should match the image a store conveys based on its exteriors. For example, if an exclusive jewelry store communicates an upscale image through an appealing shopping window–design strategy, a customer will perceive the store as unbalanced if the visual merchandising strategy inside the store does not convey that same upscale image.

The second type of balance refers to optical balance. The arrangement of all elements (e.g., fixtures, displays, checkouts) in a store should be well considered to make the overall appearance of the store harmonious and convey the impression that it is in a state of equilibrium. The easiest way to create balance in a product display is symmetry. Locating exactly the same elements on both sides of a display will render it perfectly symmetrical or even. Compared to the right side, the left side of Figure 4.14 will be perceived to be better structured and clearly arranged because the two sides of the product display include not only exactly the same products but also an equal number of products.

However, as retail space is, of course, limited and a retailer wants to present as many products as possible, products are seldom presented in

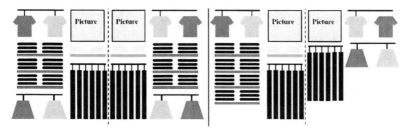

Figure 4.14. Balanced design (formal symmetry) versus unbalanced design (no symmetry).

a completely symmetrical way. Additionally, any store with a completely symmetrical merchandise layout has the risk of appearing rigid and static.[28] There is another possibility to create a balanced product presentation: informal balance. That balance can be achieved by locating different items on both sides of a vertical line, as long as these items have nearly the same optical weight or size (see Figure 4.15).[29]

Such asymmetric arrangements of merchandise can also be perceived as beautiful and appealing because the same amount of space is allocated to both sides of the wall.[30] However, not just symmetry of space conveys an attractive appearance. The number of products presented is an important aspect as well. Indeed, it makes a difference whether each product category is represented by the same number of products. At the same time, we also need to keep in mind that sales results can be strongly influenced by allocating more display space to a particular brand. For example, a study conducted in a supermarket revealed that sales increased by 44% when the display space for hard fruits was doubled.[31] For this reason, it makes sense to allocate more display space to products or brands with high profit margins. In the end, in-store design profit trumps beauty,

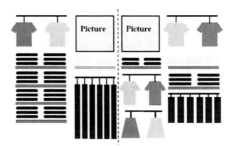

Figure 4.15. Balanced design produces informal symmetry.

even if artistically inclined visual merchandisers and window dressers may sometimes deplore this development.

Nevertheless, there is also a dark side to using a different amount of display space for different products. Displaying a different number of each brand can sometimes irritate the eye and cause shoppers to lose concentration and focus on the product. Therefore, it is recommended to highlight at least a few strong brands with an equal number of other brands (see Figure 4.16). This presentation method will positively influence the idea of perceived variety in a well-organized assortment and, in turn, their consumption rates.[32]

Rhythm: It Leads the Shopper's Eyes

Rhythm is not just an important property of music. In the context of visual merchandising, rhythm makes consumers perceive a store as well structured. Rhythm is important because it leads a customer's eyes from one item to another in a specific manner or order, enabling control of a shopper's eye movements.

Human beings recognize objects based on their experience.[33] You can use this experience to create rhythm. For example, when sorting merchandise by color, you should start with the brightest color and get darker, finally ending with the darkest color. Having the experience of a rainbow in mind, people will try to see all colors of a picture, and consequently, all your merchandise will be noticed. Another possibility for creating rhythm is by repetition. By locating the same display or the same item several times in a specific order, customers will not only walk along these paths but also pay increased attention to these objects when they repeat.

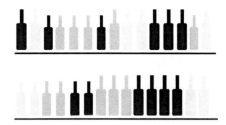

Figure 4.16. Presenting products in an unbalanced versus a balanced way.

In addition, rhythm can be created by using lines. Lines can clearly differentiate between sections of a store, inform customers where to wait in the checkout line, or guide customers through the store. Lines can also be effectively used in product displays. By connecting two products with a line, the customer's eyes will automatically follow this line. As a result, products are perceived in a specific, desired context, a fact that can have a positive impact on additional purchases. Nevertheless, not all lines have the same meaning for shoppers. Table 4.1 presents an overview of different types of lines and their likely associations.[34]

Proportion: The Mathematical Underpinnings of Beauty

The ancient Egyptians used the principle of proportion to design the pyramids, and the Greeks used it for building the Parthenon, the temple they dedicated to the Greek goddess Athena. The Taj Mahal followed the rule as well, and you can see it again when you look at the Notre Dame Cathedral in Paris. In light of the popularity and fame of these works of art, the builders did things right. All these buildings have one thing in common: They follow the principle of the golden section, which is also known as the golden mean, golden ratio, or divine proportion. Each of these geometric constructions using this golden section divides a line segment at a unique point where the ratio of the whole line (C) to the largest segment (B) is the same as the ratio of the largest segment (B) to the small segment (A). In other words, applying the ratio, A is to B as B is to C (see Figure 4.17).[35]

Table 4.1. Different Lines Used in Visual Merchandising and Their Shopper Associations

Type of business	Vision statement
Vertical lines	• **Associations:** Height, strength, dignity, formality, masculinity • **Possible use:** Basketball department of a sports store or in the men's fashion department
Diagonal lines	• **Associations:** Restlessness, dynamic, activity, instability • **Possible use:** Extreme sports stores
Horizontal lines	• **Associations:** Relaxation, safety • **Possible use:** Checkout area
Curved lines	• **Associations:** Femininity, softness • **Possible use:** Stores or departments targeting women

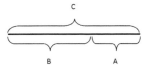

Figure 4.17. The golden ratio.

So what is the secret that lies behind this ratio? One important characteristic that always contributes to how human beings evaluate visual elements is proportion. The proportion of the golden section is exactly 1:1.62 (phi). Therefore, when a bouquet of flowers, a product display, an advertisement, a poster, or even a building have the same correct proportions, they are perceived as more aesthetically pleasing.

These proportions can be used within specific departments of a store. For example, for in-store graphics, we recommend using pictures in line with the golden section. Likewise, tables, shelves, or other elements should match the given proportions of the golden section as well.

Distance: Product Displays Should Look Great From Every Angle

Human beings strive to process visual stimuli as a whole entity.[36] Therefore, both the store and the products displayed in that store should convey a harmonious picture from every distance and view. Each element should look good when the customer enters the store as well as when customers stand directly in front of a feature wall. To achieve this effect, the whole store can be divided into different areas, and each area then represents another function (see Figure 4.18):[37]

- *Ceiling zone.* The ceiling zone is located over the shelves. All information placed in the ceiling zone can be noticed from far away. Therefore, this zone can be used to help customers orient themselves in the store. By providing large graphics or signage, customers are informed which product types they will find in a particular area. For example, supermarkets can use danglers to guide shoppers through the different aisles, indicating that a shopper will find frozen foods in one area of the store and pet food in another. In a department store, in-store graphics can

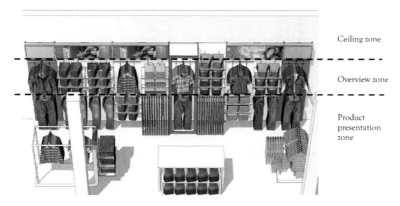

Ceiling zone

Overview zone

Product
presentation
zone

Figure 4.18. A ceiling zone, overview zone, and product presentation zone (in a three-pronged effect to exhibit the whole store).

show women shoppers that they will find women's wear in a specific department.

- *Overview zone.* The overview zone can be viewed clearly from a maximum distance of 20 feet. Merchandise identification should allow customers to see clearly the products they will find in this zone. In general, as the name indicates, this zone aims at providing an overview of the assortment in a particular department. For instance, in a fashion store, the overview zone should clearly indicate which type of women's wear shoppers can expect in a particular department (e.g., casual, business, and sportswear).

- *Product presentation zone.* Finally, products are presented in a product presentation zone. Shoppers will not see what is actually presented in this zone unless they stand right in front of the product shelf. Here the shopper will find products in various types and different sizes. In order to make as many products visible as possible, in many types of stores they should be presented with increasing height from the middle of the room toward the wall. The feature wall serves as a backdrop for each department and represents the prime visual merchandise space. Colors, lighting, in-store graphics, and different presentation methods should make this main area of merchandising space as appealing as possible. Because of its resemblance to an amphitheater or a sports arena, this type of product presentation is also called the "arena principle."

Complex Versus Simple

The overall goal when presenting your merchandise is to guide customers to find what they are looking for in a store. There are few things that are more annoying for shoppers than not to find what they are looking for. A merchandise strategy that is too complex will negatively influence the overall clarity of the store. Therefore, how products are presented should be very easily comprehendible. That clarity of product arrangement will be enhanced by striving to follow a clear structure. For example, if merchandise is arranged by colors, this strategy should be used in the whole store and not just for one display (see Figure 4.19).

Takeaway Points

Here are the most important takeaway points from this chapter:

- A good merchandising strategy can have a significant effect on sales.
- Shoppers will buy only when merchandise is visible, tangible, and accessible.
- The scarcity principle will make products more desirable, but it should be used cautiously and in moderation.

Figure 4.19. Merchandise clearly arranged by color.

- A clearly arranged assortment structure combined with highlighted products allows a retailer to offer a large variety of products while simultaneously reducing the risk of choice overload.
- Bundled presentations, which present products in their usage context, improve product evaluation and boost unplanned purchases. Include props in these bundled presentations to make this presentation technique even more effective.
- Planograms are a useful tool to implement a visual merchandising strategy.
- New and contrasting stimuli can act as eye-catchers in a store.
- In-store graphics can be used to tap into the shoppers' emotions. Most successful in this regard are schema-invoking pictures, which can be used to create specific emotional experiences.
- Archetypes and pictures triggering biologically programmed reactions will lead to particularly strong emotional experiences in the largest number of shoppers, as their effect is independent of individual experiences.
- Balance complexity with simplicity. Complexity can be achieved by combining different elements, shapes, and colors, while simplicity is characterized by using symmetry, repetition, and sequence.
- Displays should be arranged to apply the principles of rhythm and proportion.
- Arrange merchandise with a ceiling zone, overview zone, and product presentation zone in mind.

CHAPTER 5

Store Atmosphere

Communicating Using the Senses

It's a hot and stuffy summer day in Central Florida. A visibly agitated customer stands in front of the window of the customer service center at the entrance to Walt Disney World's EPCOT Center. The man is furious because of the inattentive service he received in one of the restaurants on the property, and he yells at the customer service representative behind the window. The customer service representative remains calm and asks the customer to enter the customer service lounge. A buzzer sounds, the door opens, and the angry customer enters the lounge.

The atmosphere in the lounge is very different from the rest of EPCOT Center. Instead of the heat outside, it is pleasantly air-conditioned. Soothing music plays through hidden speakers in the ceiling. The music is soft, almost imperceptible, yet clearly different from the loud, upbeat music in the rest of the park. The lounge is relatively dark, illuminated only by diffused light, while shaded windows keep the harsh sunlight out. Only a few pictures hang on the walls, and none of them show any mouse ears or any other reminders of a possible stressful experience in the theme park. Soft wall-to-wall carpeting and comfortable overstuffed chairs and sofas in muted colors complement the relaxing, serene atmosphere of the lounge.

The enraged customer is kept waiting for a few minutes, sipping a cool soft drink while seated on the comfortable sofa. When the customer representative arrives after this short cooling-off period, the guest is visibly relaxed, in a better mood, and ready to constructively discuss his complaint.

Let's analyze what happened in this situation. Before the customer entered the waiting lounge, he was extremely upset. However, after spending a few minutes in the relaxing lounge, his mood changed, and instead of shouting and making the service representative responsible for everything that went wrong that day, he is able to discuss his complaint in a constructive way. As can be seen from this example, the atmosphere of the environment strongly influences how we feel.

Atmosphere Influences How We Feel

There are many situations where other people try to influence our mood by altering the atmosphere of the environment; probably you have already done the same. For example, let us imagine that a man is in the unfortunate situation where he forgot his wedding anniversary. The man tries to rescue the situation by preparing a self-cooked, candlelit dinner for his wife with romantic background music.

Whether or not he is aware of it, a candlelit dinner is a fantastic way to influence a person's mood. When the man's wife enters the room, she is surprised by the delicious aroma of the outstanding dinner he has prepared. The low-level light of the candle puts her in a relaxed spirit. And finally, romantic music does the rest to make the wife willing to accept the husband's apology for the mistake. So scent, light, and music can clearly influence our mood. And as the old saying goes, the way to a man's heart is through his stomach. Although the saying refers to men, the same holds true for women. So the great meal certainly helped. We would like to add that the other four senses (sight, smell, touch, and hearing) are equally useful at winning a man's, a woman's, or indeed a shopper's heart.

The potential for influencing individuals through the five senses is well known by marketers. In general, when talking about how to influence shoppers through the five senses, retailers refer to the term "store atmosphere" or "atmospherics." Indeed, store atmosphere has more immediate effects on a customer's in-store behavior than do other marketing tools and techniques (such as advertising), which are not present at the point of sale.[1] Savvy retailers follow this approach to influence the buying behavior of their shoppers. For example, when entering a Victoria's Secret store, shoppers are welcomed by a warmly smiling shop assistant, the scent of pleasant potpourri enters the customer's nose, and soft music makes them feel at ease (see Figure 5.1).

Figure 5.1. Influencing the shopper through the use of the senses.

As this example shows, similar to the candlelit dinner, the five senses can be used in a retail context as well. Before providing some general guidelines how such an appealing store atmosphere can be created, we want to mention two key points:

1. *Make sure that shoppers are able to experience the intended store atmosphere.* When retailers create a pleasant store environment, they have to focus not only on the (internal) store environment but also on the external environment. Imagine a bakery where scents of fresh-baked pastries allure shoppers. In addition, soothing music plays in the background, and warm light creates a pleasant atmosphere. All in all, the bakery seems to do things right. Most of us will perceive this bakery as a very enjoyable place. However, the manipulation of atmospherics does not assure you that customers actually perceive them. To make shopping even more comfortable, every time a customer enters the bakery, the door opens automatically. Of course, during rush hour, many customers visit the store; therefore, the door is more often open than closed. Unfortunately, every time the door opens, the street noise outside drowns out the relaxing background music, and the street odors makes the perception of the fresh-bakery scent

impossible. In the early morning as well as in the evening, a glaring streetlamp shines into the bakery, eliminating the effect of warm light as well.

Admittedly, this is an extreme example, but the point is a good one, namely, that you need to ensure your customers are able to perceive the atmospheric tools you employ. In addition, elements of a store's atmosphere should be adjusted to the immediate neighborhood. If a store is located in a shopping mall where loud music is played, it does not make sense to try to drown out the music of the mall. Instead, shoppers will appreciate relaxing background music being played in the store.

2. *Show consideration for store employees.* The store atmosphere influences more than just shoppers. Indeed, every person present in the store is influenced. Particular focus should be given to the sales staff. Store employees are an important determinant of a pleasant store environment. By their interaction with shoppers, they are in a key position to influence them. If the store atmosphere has a negative impact on employees, these negative feelings will be conveyed to the customers.[2] As a case in point, take Christmas music playing in stores. It can put shoppers in a holiday mood (read, "buying gifts") but—if the songs are not changed frequently—eventually that music may be strongly resented by store clerks who are exposed only to *Jingle Bells* and *White Christmas* for days on end.

A Simple Model Can Explain Environmental Influences

In order to use store atmosphere to enhance purchase rates, it is helpful to address the question of how that store atmosphere affects shopping behavior in a more detailed way. Two environmental psychologists, Albert Mehrabian and James Russell, developed a simple model that explains how individuals react to a specific environment. The basic proposition of the Mehrabian-Russell model is that a shopper's behavior is influenced by the environment. However, this influence on behavior is not direct. Instead, the environment (the store) influences a shopper's emotions and mood, which in turn influence the shopper's behavior.[3] Let's look at the variables in the model (see Figure 5.2) one by one.

Figure 5.2. The Mehrabian-Russell model.

There are two determinants of a certain behavior: personality variables and environmental variables. Let's first focus on the environmental variables.

Environmental Variables

Every stimulus in our environment can act as an environmental variable, which then causes a specific behavior. For example, the music or the scent in a store may provoke a certain reaction. Among other variables, both of these stimuli influence a shopper's arousal level. Arousal can be described as feeling excited, stimulated, and activated. In a retail setting, shoppers can easily get bored if the arousal level is too low. The sum of all the environmental variables surrounding you as a consumer is called "information rate."[4] This information rate can be characterized, on the one hand, by the complexity of the stimuli and, on the other hand, by their novelty. Whether shoppers will perceive the information rate as high or low depends on these two characteristics:

1. *Novelty* refers to new stimuli in the store environment. Remember a situation where you entered a store for the first time? At that first moment, you might be utterly impressed by the store design and the beautifully arranged products. After visiting the shop several times, you will probably be less impressed by these environmental factors, as you already know them.

2. *Complexity* does not depend on the number of previous visits to the store but on the arrangement of environmental factors in the store. Some environments can be processed easily, while others cannot. The complexity of a store depends on several factors (e.g., the number of products offered, how different these products are, the size of the store, the number of people [shoppers and employees] in the store, and so on).

In summary, all environmental stimuli can be characterized according to their degree of novelty and complexity. Retailers can use these two characteristics to either enhance or reduce the information rate of an environment, which in turn directly affects the arousal level of shoppers.

Personality Variables

However both environmental factors and personality variables cause specific behaviors. It depends on a shopper's personality type (i.e., whether that person will perceive the information rate as being high or low). In general, consumers can be either arousal seekers or arousal avoiders:

- *Arousal seekers* appreciate exciting store environments. They like to try new things and want to have their shopping trip be an adventure. For this target group, the information rate should be rather high. Customers should be surprised with changed store environments and arousing environmental stimuli (intensive scent, loud music, bright colors).
- *Arousal avoiders* can be easily characterized as the opposite of arousal seekers. They try to avoid exposure to too many external stimuli and appreciate a calm, relaxing shopping atmosphere. If a store's target group is mainly characterized by arousal avoiders, you should keep the information rate at a lower level.

Drivers of Behavior: Arousal, Pleasure, and Dominance

Until now, we have discussed the variables at the very left of the model. The information rate (all environmental stimuli), as well as personality variables, influences consumer behavior. However, this influence is not direct. How shoppers react to a store depends on their affective state:

- Arousal-nonarousal
- Pleasure-displeasure
- Dominance-submissiveness

Arousal refers to excited, stimulating, and activating feelings. Pleasure refers to being in a good mood and feeling joyful. And, finally, dominance stands for feeling unrestricted and able to act in a variety of ways. Since arousal and pleasure are the most important drivers of shopper behavior in a store, we focus on these two emotional dimensions here.

Arousal and Pleasure

Arousal has an important influence on a customer's store evaluation. Indeed, whether patrons decide to stay in a store or leave depends significantly on the arousal level elicited by the store. Arousal represents not just an important concept in a retail context. It is the basis for all processes in the human organism. The extent to which a specific arousal level is perceived as pleasurable depends on the individual. Arousal seekers will be delighted by the idea of bungee jumping, while arousal avoiders could not imagine anything worse. Nevertheless, there is a point where a high arousal level turns into panic. In contrast, if a person experiences the lowest arousal level, he will be in a deep sleep.

The different states of arousal can be described by an inverted U-shape, illustrated in Figure 5.3. At the far-left end, as well as at the far-right end, the performance level (human's processing capacity) is at its lowest point, either because the person is in deep sleep (very left end) or because she is overstrained by too many stimuli, resulting in unpleasant feelings and, in the worst case, panic (the far-right end). The optimum arousal level is at the highest peak of the curve. Individuals experiencing that optimum arousal level are alert and receptive to environmental stimuli (such as sales

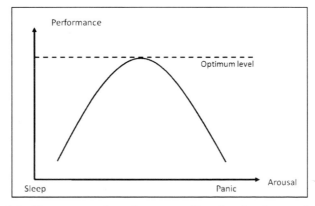

Figure 5.3. Shoppers perform best at medium levels of arousal, also known as the optimum level.

signs or product displays). Obviously, a retailer should try to evoke this optimal arousal level in shoppers.

In general, shoppers in an arousal-stimulating atmosphere show a more positive store assessment and desirable in-store behavior.[5] In fact, consumers often spend more time in arousing stores due to having a more interesting store environment when the store atmosphere is arousal inducing.[6]

Nevertheless, there is still the question about the degree to which retailers should increase the arousal level of their customers. This degree may vary depending on the specific shopping situation. In many instances it is advantageous to increase the arousal level of shoppers. For example, going shopping at the mall at 10:00 a.m. on a Monday morning is usually not very exciting. There are few customers in the mall, as well as no entertainment. In this environment, it is useful to increase the shoppers' arousal level (e.g., by using bright lighting and fast music).

There are, however, also situations when steps need to be taken to reduce shoppers' arousal state because the optimal state of arousal has clearly been exceeded. Just think back to the last days before Christmas. Although we know that the day will come when all shops are closed and we want to please our family and friends with thoughtful gifts, occasionally we realize only a few days before Christmas that we still need to buy presents. Most of us will then meet in overcrowded malls and stores and fight for the last presents. Although the mall or the store usually evokes pleasant feelings, the extremely high arousal level of this situation has the opposite effect on these last-minute Christmas shoppers.

So what can a retailer do to avoid such reactions? You can use specific stimuli not only to increase the arousal level but also to decrease it. For example, water has a relaxing effect on individuals. For that reason water features are often used in shopping malls and stores. Similarly, plants can be used to decrease the arousal level of your customers. Often, malls provide calm zones with seats surrounded by plants that enable the customer to relax and find new energy to continue the shopping trip. A great example is an outdoor mall south of Miami (Figure 5.4) where a river literally runs through it. After following the meandering brook and the swaying palm trees from one store to the next, even the most strung out shoppers will start to relax and enjoy their shopping experience.

Figure 5.4. Water and plants are deactivating stimuli that create a relaxed atmosphere at an outdoor mall.

Likewise, a store can use arousal-inducing as well as arousal-reducing stimuli to create an optimal atmosphere in terms of arousal. There are two strategies:[7]

1. Use arousal inducing and reducing stimuli simultaneously.
2. Create contrasting zones in a single store.

The first strategy aims at evoking an optimal arousal level by combining the two kinds of stimuli at the same time. For example, the store can use a clearly structured (arousal reducing) but new store layout (arousal inducing). Similarly, a store can use low lighting (arousal reducing) for products placed in an unusual, surprising location (arousal inducing).[8]

The second strategy uses these two kinds of stimuli as well, but in different zones of the store. Although shoppers appreciate arousing stimuli, they strive afterward for relaxing and calming stimuli. A store can provide arousing zones with dazzling colors, bright lighting, and loud music, while other areas aim at giving customers feelings of relaxation by using pastel colors, dim lighting, and soothing music.

There are some general characteristics of a store that a retailer can consciously change to increase or decrease the arousal level of customers. Table 5.1 offers an overview of such arousal increasing and arousal reducing stimuli.

Table 5.1. Arousing-Inducing Versus Arousal-Reducing Stimuli

Arousal-inducing stimuli	Arousal-reducing stimuli
Large space, bright store illumination, bright colors, and fast and loud music	Discreet lighting, small room size, and discreet music
Visual cues showing emotional situations, arousing scents, and loud music	Visual cues showing nature, relaxing music, plants, and natural lighting
Novel, surprising, and exceptional store design	Familiar, structured, and clearly arranged store design

Sources: Berlyne (1971); Bost (1987).

Until now, we have only discussed the arousal that can be evoked by external stimuli. However, the second relevant mood state (pleasure) should not be neglected. Certainly, we want to evoke positive feelings in our customers. So the crucial question is, how can this positivity be accomplished? To answer this question, it makes sense to regard store atmosphere as a combination of pleasure and arousal. In fact, environments can be classified based on these two dimensions (see Figure 5.5).

An environment can be sleepy or arousing and pleasant or unpleasant. An arousing retail environment does not automatically mean that a shopper feels comfortable. In addition, not all pleasant environments are arousing. When spending a relaxing evening in a nice restaurant, usually there is no high level of arousal experience; nevertheless, the evening will be enjoyable. So the crucial question is, what do you want to achieve with your store atmosphere? On which dimension (or, better, between which dimensions) would you place your store? Figure 5.5 will help you position your store so you achieve the right balance between arousal and relaxation. As a matter of course, a store should not be placed between unpleasant and sleepy. A store with an appealing atmosphere has to be located on the right side of the scale, evoking either arousing in combination with pleasant feelings (e.g., sports store, music store) or nonarousing in combination with pleasant feelings (e.g., wine store, bookstore).

While upscale restaurants often strive to create a nonarousing and pleasing atmosphere to allow its guests to relax, fast-food restaurants that have a need for high table turnover might use slightly uncomfortable seats and bold colors to prevent customers from lingering. In retailing, it is usually advisable to evoke positive feelings in shoppers. In fact, happy customers buy more. For example, research has shown that happy customers tend

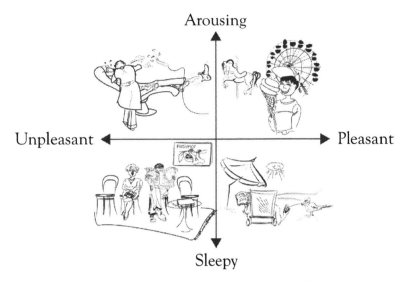

Figure 5.5. Four combinations of pleasure and arousal.

to spend more money than they originally planned.[9] Obviously, this is a behavior that retailers want to encourage. In addition, positive feelings in customers lead to several other positive outcomes. For example, happy customers have a higher probability of achieving their purchase goal. In other words, customers in a good mood find what they are looking for more often. This goal of achievement has a positive impact on consumer satisfaction.[10] In sum, by creating an appropriately high arousal level as well as a high level of pleasure, customers will do the following:

- Spend more time in the store.[11]
- Spend more money than originally planned.[12]
- Have higher patronage intentions.[13]
- Have a greater degree of satisfaction with their shopping.[14]

In order to achieve these desirable outcomes, retailers need to make their customers happy, which can be achieved with the right store atmosphere. Store atmosphere is an essential part of the store environment. It consists of a number of elements, some of which are relatively easy to control, while others are not. In the following section we discuss those factors that can be controlled within a store environment: music, scent, lighting, color, and density. Each of these elements has a considerable impact on whether approach or avoidance behavior is demonstrated by consumers.

How to Create a Favorable Store Atmosphere

When passing a store, often only a few seconds will determine whether a shopper will enter that store or not. Let us give you an example: You walk through a shopping mall when you suddenly pass an apparel store. The beautifully decorated shop window raises your attention, so you stop and glance on the displayed merchandise. The enjoyable background music enters your ears, and an almost imperceptible citrus scent comes from the entrance. You decide to spend a few minutes browsing through that store.

Visual, as well as the olfactory and the auditory stimuli, caused this approach behavior. However, much more needs to be done other than just getting customers into the store by use of various stimuli. In fact, several desirable outcomes can be evoked by the specific use of music, scent, lighting, and color.

Listen to the Music

Perhaps you know the situation. When you listen to your favorite song on the radio, your mood tends to improve. Indeed, music has an impressive effect on mood states. This same response can also be used in store design. There are numerous possibilities for varying music. For example, music can be played loud or soft, fast or slow, and be vocal or instrumental. Additionally, music can be played as background or foreground music. However, when music is played in the foreground, it is possible that the whole attention of a customer may be drawn to the music instead of the retailer's merchandise.[15] Of course, many different music styles do exist, such as lounge music, heavy rock, techno, or classical, just to name a few. Many service businesses and retailers use music to induce a specific behavior in their customers. Music played in a store can lead to several desirable reactions.

Slow Music Keeps Customers in a Store

How music tempo is consciously applied to influence consumers can once again be best demonstrated when comparing a fast-food restaurant with an exclusive restaurant. A fast-food restaurant is usually character-ized by a high arousal level: There are many people, bright lights, and loud, fast music. In contrast, the exclusive restaurant aims to create a relaxing atmosphere by providing dim light in combination with candle-light, tables are located at a comfortable distance from each other, and slow background music plays. In the fast food restaurant, loud and fast music is, among other elements, responsible for the high table turnover.[16] Customers leave right after eating their meal, which is actually intended by the restaurant. In contrast, the relaxing atmosphere of the exclusive restaurant leads customers to stay after their meal and consume high-margin items such as cocktails.[17]

Influencing customers to stay longer should also be a goal in a retail setting. In general, the longer that shoppers stay in a store, the more con-tact they will have with the products in that store, which in turn results in higher purchase rates. Slow music is an important tool to make cus-tomers spend more time in a store.[18] Slow music can also lead to a rise in purchase rates; studies have reported an increase of sales of up to 38% when slow music was played instead of fast.[19]

Music Influences Price and Quality Perceptions

There is another important effect on shopping behavior that retailers can use by playing music in the stores. Music positively influences the perception of merchandise quality, as well as of service quality. Inter-estingly, not only the music style but also the music genre produces this effect. With classical music, service quality will be more highly evaluated if the music is fast rather than slow. In contrast, when Top 40 music is played, slower music will increase quality perceptions. In addition to these two characteristics of music, consumers will evaluate products, as well as store service, higher when they actually like the music played.[20]

Retailers can influence not only quality perception but also price per-ceptions. Classical music conveys a prestigious, exclusive, and high-priced image to customers. If Top 40 music is played, shoppers will expect to find lower priced products in the store.[21]

Music Style Affects Perceived Time Spent in the Store

Research has revealed that individuals budget a certain amount of time for their shopping. When this amount of time is perceived to have elapsed, the consumer will decide to stop shopping.[22] Therefore, retailers should try to hold down the perception of time spent in the store and keep it as low as possible. Again, music is an important tool to achieve this aim. However, in this case, the type of music is the key to success. People perceive the time spent in a store as being long when they are confronted with music they do not know. For example, when a store targeting young people plays classical music in the background, the shopping time will be perceived as long (under the condition, of course, that these young people do not usually hear classical music). The same holds true when people accustomed to classical music visit a store where Top 40 music is played.[23]

Music Leads to More Interactions With Sales Staff

Music not only directly influences purchase rates but also influences other facets of consumer behavior, which in turn positively impact the likelihood of purchase. In fact, a retailer can influence the intensity of communication between salespeople and consumers by playing both slow-tempo and low-arousing music instead of high-tempo and arousing music or no music at all.[24] The willingness of customers to talk to salespeople can be enhanced by playing soothing music. This is especially useful in a service environment where the advice of salesclerks is an important sales instrument (e.g., a car dealership).

The persuasiveness of sales clerks can be enhanced by music as well. Shoppers are looking for other cues when they do not want to rely only on salespeople. With music representing such a cue, customers consider the music to be additional information when making purchase decisions.

Music Facilitates Information Recall

Maybe you have been in the situation where you hear a song on the radio and suddenly you recall a situation you might not have thought about for a long time. The process of recalling relevant information in a sales situation works in a similar way. A music-induced emotional state, which is similar to the one where the cues were encoded, facilitates the memory-retrieval process. Music does not always facilitate the recall of information, however. Only when the music fits the setting well is it easier for people to remember. In contrast, when the music does not fit, customers need more cognitive effort to remember.[25] Therefore, music can be used to recall pleasant information for customers. For example, Caribbean music in a travel agency might let people recall memories of the last holiday, putting customers in a good mood. Similarly, playing disco music in a fashion store can enhance customer's recall of their last party.

Music Can Keep an Unwanted Audience Away

While music attracts, it is also a useful tool to keep certain groups of people away from a store. For example, the manager of a convenience store had a problem with crowds of teenagers who were loitering and partying in the parking lot. The solution was to install rooftop speakers playing Mozart, Mantovani, and 1960s folk tunes. Reportedly, this music was sufficient to clear out the partiers because the teenagers hated that music. "When you pipe in Mozart or Mantovani, it's a subtle way to move kids out," he stated.[26] While we are not sure if this approach was really that subtle, it is certainly restrained compared to other methods used to reduce teenage loitering.

There are even more drastic auditory measures that can be taken. A Tokyo park has started to play an annoying, high-pitched tone at night to keep away teens who want to vandalize the park. As people's ability to hear high frequencies falls with age, only teens are able to hear this tone; older people cannot. However, in the spirit of intergenerational understanding (and to protect you from lawsuits), we advise against this strategy.[27]

How to Bring Music Into the Store

Finally, we want to have a brief look at the various ways you can bring music into your store. All differ according to the extent of control you want for the kind of music. Turning on the radio station takes the least effort; at the same time, it offers the fewest controls. Nevertheless, there are other possibilities, which we discuss in the following sections.

Turning on a Radio Station

Usually, you need a special license, depending on the country and state in which your store is located, to use the radio in your store. But this is not the only disadvantage. If you use a radio channel, you have little control over the kind of music your customers will hear. Further, the music is interrupted by radio commercials. In the worst case, these may even be commercials of your competitors. So in summary, a radio station is not recommended for use in your salesroom.

Purchasing or Renting Specialized In-Store Music CDs or MP3s

The second possibility, the purchase of CDs and MP3s, has the advantage that you have full control over the music. The music style, as well as the tempo, can be chosen by you. However, if you purchase your own CDs, you have to pay a copyright fee to the organization representing the music industry because you play them in public. Usually, there is the option to rent specialized CDs containing in-store music instead of purchasing them. This music choice has the advantage that songs are changed frequently, which prevents your customers and your staff from getting bored.

Subscribing to Satellite Stations That Transmit Background Music

You can also subscribe to a satellite station specializing in background music for stores. Satellite stations are available for many different kinds of music. Usually, the music style can be varied depending on the time of day. Of course, this is a great advantage, as it enables you to address different target groups at different times. For example, an apparel store might play adult favorites in the morning, while Top 40 music is played in the evening when school is out and the customer demographic changes.

Running Your Own In-Store Radio Station

If you want to run your own commercials and present other information about your store, an in-store radio would be appropriate. In fact, this method will provide you with the most control; however, it is also the most elaborate and thus the most costly way to get music into your store. Nevertheless, an in-store radio station has several advantages. First, it not only delivers music but also communicates with shoppers through commercials. Second, it delivers valuable information to customers so it is not perceived simply as background noise. Third, it improves the shopping experience and entertains customers. Finally, the in-store radio informs and educates not only customers but also your sales staff. By referring to the latest promotions in the in-store radio, sales personnel become better informed and thus more qualified to make sales.[28]

In sum, the purchase or rent of CDs or MP3s as well as the renting of a special radio station seem to be meaningful variants for playing music on your premises. Likewise, running your own in-store radio might be appropriate, but the associated expenditures with this choice make this a viable option only for large retail chains.

The Sweet Smell of Success

Although music does strongly impact shopping behavior, there is one stimulus that has an even stronger effect on human moods. Of the five senses, the olfactory sense has the strongest influence on emotions, as the olfactory bulb (the nerve endings that connect the nose to the brain) is directly connected to the limbic system, which is responsible for immediate emotional reactions.[29] In general, we have to distinguish between odors that are used to perfume a product and a fragrance used for an entire retail store. The latter odor is referred to as ambient scent. The main characteristic of an ambient scent is that it is not object specific. Again, there are several possibilities to vary such scents. Scents can be varied according to their affective quality (i.e., how pleasantly the scent is perceived), their arousal level, and of course their intensity.[30]

More and more retailers use scents to brand their stores. For example, the Samsung flagship stores have their own signature smell, a honeydew melon scent.[31] The goal is to make the store unique and subtly differentiate it from the competition.

Scents not only brand a store but also evoke strong emotional responses, such as the feeling of being more relaxed, peppy, or nostalgic. Through their strong impact on shopper mood, they can have many desirable effects on shopping behavior.

Improve Shopper Mood With Odors

The strong effects that ambient scents can have on shoppers' moods became evident to us when we conducted an experiment where we had shoppers evaluate the products in a lingerie store. Unbeknownst to the shoppers, we pumped either an erotic or a fresh smell into the shopping environment. While both smells were very pleasant, shoppers who smelled the erotic scent evaluated the products significantly better than did the shoppers who smelled the fresh citrus smell. In addition, the former were also in a better mood. Scents can improve shopper mood, which then makes them more likely to make purchases. However, our results showed that it is not enough to simply use a pleasant smell. The ambient scent must also be congruent—that is, it must fit the store—which explains why the pleasant erotic smell led to the desired result and the equally pleasant fresh scent in this type of store did not.[32] Because congruency plays such an important role when using odors and other atmospheric variables, we will return to this issue later in the chapter.

Attract Customers With Scents

Some scents are so appealing that they cannot fail to attract the consumer's nose. Several stores use odors to entice shoppers into their store. By addressing senses other than the visual through appealing store windows, scented stores also can attract customers. For example, specialty stores for soaps use intense fragrances to alert customers. Similarly, the smell of fresh-made bakery products from a bakery makes a customer's mouth water, encouraging them to enter the store and shop.

Encourage Shoppers to Linger

If shopping time were money, stores could gain considerable turnover rates by using pleasant odors in their store. In an experimental setting, the amount of time spent in a scented store was overestimated by 40%.[33] In contrast, people in an unscented setting stated that they felt that they spent more time in the store than they actually did. In addition, the evaluation of the store overall and the store environment was more positive in the scented setting. So it can be suggested that (subtle) scents do seem to positively affect the time people spend in a store, as well as their overall evaluation of that store.[34]

Smell to Sell

Interestingly, the impressive effect of spending behavior becomes more obvious in a gambling setting. In one Las Vegas casino, gamblers spent more money at the slot machines in a scented environment than in an unscented environment.[35] The influence of odors on individual spending behavior can also be seen in a more conventional retail environment. Indeed, specialty shops like coffee roasters use this tool to create a purchase-inducing atmosphere. Cigar shops, secondhand bookshops, and bakeries support the natural fragrance of their products by releasing additional scents to the air.[36] Products are more positively evaluated in a scented setting that fits the store type, resulting in higher purchase rates. However, when using ambient scents, one should consider that the fragrance has to support all the products; otherwise, the increase in the purchase of one fragranced product will jeopardize all the other products.[37] Therefore, instead of using a product-specific scent, it is better to use an appealing scent that is suitable for the whole store and all the products.

We found such a scent for one of our clients, a chain of pastry shops. There we tried out a scent scrumptiously called "Cookies & Cream." The scent was emitted in one of the stores on alternating days. What was the effect on sales? You guessed it: There was indeed a (modest) increase in sales on the days the scent was put in the air.

Did you know that an average person is capable of smelling about 10,000 different kinds of odors?[38] Don't worry. There is no need to try all of them. Instead, we put together a short overview of the most effective scents used in retail settings for you (see Table 5.2).

Table 5.2. General Responses to Different Scents

Scent	Response
Lavender, basil, cinnamon	Relaxing, results in soothing energy levels, calming
Peppermint, thyme, rosemary, grapefruit, eucalyptus	Increases arousal level, energizing and stimulating, increases productivity
Orange, lavender	Reduces anxiety (e.g., in a dental office)
Ginger, chocolate, cardamom, licorice	Evokes feelings of romance
Floral scents	Increases time spent in a mall
Vanilla	Comforts, gives warm sense of home and hearth, calming
Black pepper	Sexually stimulating

Sources: Hunter (1995); Lehrner et al. (2005); Lovelock and Wirtz (2011); Mattila and Wirtz (2001).

Irrespective of which scent is used, the level of intensity matters. If too intense an odor is used, consumers will become irritated. Nevertheless, to influence customers, the intensity must be able to be perceived. The intensity of scents can be well explained by the inverted U-shape we mentioned earlier when talking about arousal. On the one hand, a less intense scent will evoke no arousal, and on the other, a too intense scent will bother people. For example, a shoe shop can use smells of leather to animate customers to buy. Nevertheless, if the smell is too intense, shoppers will be distracted from the products as they find the odor to be unpleasant.[39] From our experience, the level of intensity of an ambient scent is usually right if most shoppers don't consciously notice it when they enter the store but can still perceive the smell when asked about it.

The amount of scent can be easily controlled by the various technical devices you can use to bring the odor into your store. We present them at the end of this section.

Although the effect of different scents has been investigated, the response to scent depends, in the end, on the individual. While some people like lavender, others will associate negative experiences with this fragrance. Therefore, it is useful to identify those scents that evoke positive feelings in all of us. This task led us to conduct a study that examined the effect of human pheromones on consumer behavior. Pheromones are body scents produced by human beings, and these fragrances are completely natural and perceived very similarly by many people. In the study we used a male pheromone called androstenol, which has a slightly musky, but pleasant, scent. Our study revealed some interesting findings. Indeed, it is possible to influence the perception of products with human pheromones. Men perceived masculine products as even more masculine when they made their evaluations while smelling the male pheromone.[40] Only men were influenced by the male pheromone, while women were resistant to it in the store, as these pheromones are commonly thought as scents of sexual attraction. Nature works in wondrous ways.

Releasing Scents in the Air

Although we have discussed several ways scents can be used to create a pleasant store atmosphere and, in turn, influence consumer behavior, we have not dealt with the question of how these scents should be diffused into the air. In fact, there is such a huge demand for ambient odors that scent-marketing companies are now available. Although we do not want to go into scent procedures in detail, we do want to introduce the most common ways that scents are disseminated in a store.

In general, one should distinguish between stand-alone devices used for releasing scents to the air and systems installed in the store's ventilator system. Obviously, the decision between these two options depends mainly on store size. For smaller stores, there are flexible devices that can release odors either by atomization (electrical sprayers that release scents at predetermined time intervals) or by vaporization. Some companies also offer a surface-mounting solution, which makes the scent devices completely invisible to customers.

Putting Your Store in the Right Light

In-store illumination is also an important determinant of store atmosphere. When entering a store, our first impression is often influenced by the available light. Have you ever bought food at a discount store? The lighting of the store not only influences the in-store behavior of the customer but also acts as a cue. While discount stores are usually brightly illuminated, aiming to make their customers buy efficiently, department stores use lower light levels to induce a relaxed feeling. Although lighting is only a part of the overall atmosphere, it has a considerable influence on human behavior. Again, the Mehrabian-Russell model we introduced earlier can be used to explain how lighting impacts individuals. It is assumed that bright rooms will lead to a higher arousal level than dimly lighted ones.[41] Numerous desirable reactions on the part of the consumer can be caused by the right light:

- *A bright light setting increases impulse purchases.* Light can have an impact on impulse purchases. Bright light settings will increase an individual's level of arousal, which in turn will increase the propensity to make impulse purchases. However, again it should be noted that a certain level of arousal should not be exceeded; otherwise, avoidance behavior will occur instead of approach behavior. An individual prefers illumination levels that produce optimal levels of arousal. However,

lighting should be varied in a sensible way, as insufficient lighting will hinder customers visually.[42]

- *Light has a positive effect on items being handled.* Bright lighting
  has a positive effect on items examined and also on the number of items handled in a retail store.[43] Overall lighting will
  positively impact not only the number of products examined
  but also how attractive these products appear. Consumers will
  spend more time in front of a lighted display than they will in
  front of an unlighted display.[44]

Displays can be illuminated separately. There are many different
zones in a store that require special kinds of light. You should consider
the quality of light needed for each application. For example, a bookstore will generally be brightly illuminated, but to make your customers
use and enjoy the reading corner, you should reduce the brightness in
the overall store and increase the brightness in the reading areas (see
Figure 5.6).

Similarly, you can use different lighting to highlight merchandise. Use
lower lights for the walls and floors, but use brighter lights for your products. You can choose between five various possibilities:[45]

Figure 5.6. Increase the brightness of the reading areas in a
bookstore.

1. *General lighting* (see Figure 5.7a) refers to how the whole store is illuminated. There is no focus on a product or a special wall. In other words, this lighting is just background illumination. It should be bright enough to enable shoppers to browse through the entire store.

2. If you want to lead shoppers through the whole store, a *linear lighting system* (see Figure 5.7b) will help your customers find their way. Linear lighting is placed over the main aisles or main loop of the store, while other lighting systems are used for the rest of the store.

3. Light can (and should) be used to highlight products. Depending on the way you present your merchandise, either *directional lighting* (see Figure 5.7c) can be used to direct a light beam to the fixture or you can use a *point light system* (see Figure 5.7d) to highlight certain products.

4. In some cases, a *baffled light* (see Figure 5.7e) will flatter your merchandise. Products are not illuminated directly but rather indirectly with the use of an additional material, such as wood or metal.

5. Finally, the fixture you use for the presentation of merchandise can be illuminated itself. This is called *specialty lighting* (see Figure 5.7f). You will often find this lighting concept in jewelry stores, where it makes the jewelry shine and sparkle.

In addition, you can create useful optical illusions with lighting. For example, a store can seem larger by projecting light on the walls

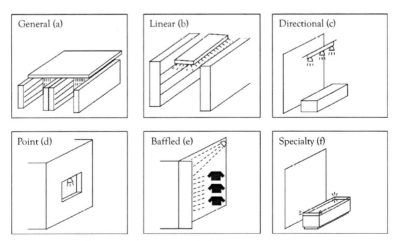

Figure 5.7. Different lighting possibilities.

or by increasing the ceiling brightness. Likewise, if a store has low ceilings, you can use wall-washing lights on a light-colored surface to make them appear higher. Similarly, high ceilings can be made optically lower through the use of pendant lights with project illumination. Isn't it amazing what you can do with lights?

But we are not finished. You can also make small or narrow stores look bigger through the specific use of lights. If you have a narrow room, project light on it in combination with bright wall colors. You can use the same idea if the store is too wide. Then you should use dark colors and not project the light on the whole wall, but only on the products you want to highlight.[46]

In fact, by playing with the light (i.e., by varying the use of shadow or direct light), you can evoke certain feelings in your customer. For example, soft, flowing light and zones with subdued lighting have a calming and relaxing impact on shoppers.[47]

Different lighting zones will also help your customers orient themselves in the store. When planning a lighting concept, be aware that light always interacts with colors. For example, red-colored store elements illuminated with a blue light lets these store elements be perceived as violet. Therefore, when considering a certain color for store use, both natural and artificial light need to be evaluated.

Color Up Your Store

Colors are such a self-evident part of our lives that we take them for granted. Indeed, we do not think about why we like some colors more and some colors less or not at all. Nevertheless, we expect certain stores to have certain colors. While the Apple store usually uses white for its interiors, Starbucks utilizes dark green and brown shades. Indeed, certain colors evoke different associations. Table 5.3 can be a starting point when choosing colors for your store. Just keep in mind that color associations are to a large extent influenced by culture. While the symbolic meanings of colors shown in the table hold true in Western societies (i.e., the United States and Europe), in other parts of the world, many associations are different. Furthermore, color associations differ across various target groups (e.g., men vs. women, teenagers vs. older consumers).

Table 5.3. Common Color Associations

Color	Association
White	Purity, cleanliness, refinement, coldness, mainly positive associations
Black	Quite often negative emotions, such as mourning or unhappiness, but also elegance, high quality, power, masterfulness
Yellow	Cheer, freshness, vitality, a warm and comfortable atmosphere
Green	Nature, hope, calmness, relaxation, freshness, health, freedom
Blue	Calmness, prettiness, security, harmony, friendship, helpfulness, security, comfort, authority
Red	Excitement, stimulation, either positive (love, passion) or negative (anger), vitality, activity, novelty, but also aggression and strength
Orange	Power, affordability, informality
Brown	Stability, security, everyday life, domesticity, wood, trees, earth
Gold	Elegance, exclusiveness, power, wealth
Silver	Femininity, coldness, inaccessibility, ceremony, simplicity, distance

Sources: Wexner (1954); Angermann (1989); Kanner (1989).

Because of their symbolic meanings, colors play an important role in retail branding. Additionally, colors can be used to easily create an appealing store atmosphere. In addition to the culture-bound associations that people make with various colors, individuals also react to colors with certain automatic biological responses. In other words, there is little individual difference between persons in terms of their biological reaction to colors.[48]

To find out how colors affect consumer behavior, we have to address two questions: What color? And what affect? Of course we can't make a general statement about how colors affect shopping behavior. We do have to consider which color we want to use. Likewise, we have to think about which behavior we want to achieve. Similar to the Mehrabian-Russell model, two different emotional effects can be achieved by using color. These effects can be classified based on two dimensions:

1. *Pleasure.* This response deals with a consumer's feeling of well-being. It is mainly based on whether we like the color we see.
2. *Arousal.* Some colors enhances a consumer's arousal level, while others have an adverse effect

In other words, whether a color enhances a customer's enjoyment of a certain stimulus is mostly independent of the activating or deactivating effect of that color.[49] Therefore, when discussing colors, we have to distinguish arousal from the affective response to the color. Based on these two dimensions, different consumer responses can be evoked by the use of color.

Create Peacefulness or Excitement

In general, warm colors produce excitement, while cool colors cause peacefulness and relaxation. However, you can evoke different mood states not only with different kinds of colors but also with different intensities of those. In fact, bright colors are usually perceived as attractive, while dull colors tend to be perceived as uncomfortable.[50]

Colors can also be characterized according to their wavelengths, with violet on one end of the continuum and red on the other (see Figure 5.8).

Blue colors are considered cool colors, as they are characterized by a short wavelength. Red-tone colors have a long wavelength and are perceived as warm colors.[51]

Enhance Overall Store Evaluation

With this empirical evidence in mind, how can we use colors to influence shopping behavior? In general, blue-colored stores are evaluated more positively compared to red-colored stores.[52] In contrast to blue, red is the least preferred color in a store setting and leads to the worst evaluation of a store. Nevertheless, like blue, red also has positive effects. A red-colored store environment enhances impulse buying. This is because red is the most activating color.[53]

However, in general, customers prefer blue retail environments (and blue is also the favorite color of most consumers). Table 5.4 presents some impressive empirical findings about the influence of color on shoppers in a retail environment.

Figure 5.8. The dimensions of color.

Table 5.4. Effects of a Blue Versus a Red Store Environment

Blue retail environment	Red retail environment
• More favorable store evaluation	• Less favorable store evaluation
• Greater shopping intention	• Lower excitement and perceived price fairness
• Greater purchase intention	• Lower patronage and purchase intention
	• More impulse purchases

Increase Impulse Purchase Rates

In general, we recommend focusing on low-wavelength colors. However, in some situations, a red environment will also increase your sales. Indeed, it has been revealed that merchandise is perceived as more up-to-date if it is presented in a red environment. Hence you should use red if you want to enhance impulse buying and if you sell stylish merchandise.

Put Customers in a Relaxed Spirit

In contrast, green should be avoided in impulse-buying situations. Green is an appropriate color for a situation in which a lower activation level is required, such as waiting in lines. If the main focus of your business is to create a positive attitude toward your store, shorter wavelength colors (e.g., blue) are more appropriate. Sometimes it's more meaningful to create a pleasant atmosphere instead of trying to heighten impulse-purchase rates. At exclusive restaurants and upscale jewelry stores, it is more meaningful to use blue, as blue will evoke pleasurable feelings in your customers.[54]

To summarize, colors are a fantastic tool to use to influence the behavior of your customers. However, colors should be used to a meaningful degree; otherwise, overuse will lead to avoidance instead of approach behavior because of color overstimulation. Colors, like all store elements, have to be considered in combination with other elements. For example, a violet wall will appear completely different when illuminated with a blue or a red light. We will take a deeper look on the combinations of such different atmospheric elements later in this section.

Crowding: Give Your Customers
Enough Breathing Space

In addition to all the atmospheric elements mentioned already, there's one more factor that will influence store atmosphere: perceived crowding. Crowding refers to a state of psychological stress that occurs when an individual's demand for space exceeds the perceived supply of space. This stress could happen either because a store is simply too small, because too many people are present in the store, or simply because of personal anxiety.

Density is the key determinant of crowding. However, high density does not automatically lead to a negative judgment of a store. As with all other environmental variables, density can act as either a positive or a negative cue. Would you like to have dinner in a restaurant with no guests? Most of us would infer that the restaurant might not be the best choice, since the number of guests in a restaurant has an impact on its perceived quality. However, in the case of crowding, the perception of density leads to negative outcomes. Have you ever been in a situation where you entered a store and the first thought you had was to leave it again as quickly as possible, as there were so many other people in the store that you felt claustrophobic? High-density conditions result in lower satisfaction[55] and less desire to stay in the shop, browse through it, or contact salespeople.[56] In addition, when products are bought in a perceived high-density environment, customers show a lower level of satisfaction with the purchased items.[57]

Crowding should definitely be avoided by retailers. There are certain suggestions we can give you to reduce the risk of crowding:

- *Enough space for well-attended store zones.* Consumers might perceive density even though a store is not actually crowded. Individuals have different limits for their crowding perception. Therefore, enough space should be allocated to zones in a store where many customers meet each other. Such zones include primarily the entrance and checkout zones, as well as the information desks, service bars, or aisles where frequently sought products are located.

- *Wide aisles.* Wide aisles are important to avoid crowding situations, especially in stores where shopping carts are used. However, shopping carts are not the only things that need enough space to be maneuvered through aisles. Stores targeting families have to consider the space needed for baby carriages or strollers. Older people might use walkers or wheelchairs, which also require wide aisles.
- *Clearly arranged store layout.* People standing disoriented in a store and thinking where they have to go next can hinder other customers who wish to move quickly to their desired aisle. Therefore, a clearly arranged store layout will maintain consistent customer flow and avoid these human barriers.
- *Slow-tempo music.* Having many people in a store will increase the arousal level of customers. However, in this situation there is also the risk of evoking too high an arousal level, even a state of panic. Therefore, a store should aim to reduce customer arousal to a comfortable level by playing slow-tempo music. Customers will feel calm and relaxed and, as a result, perceive a situation as being less crowded.

Congruence: All Stimuli Must Match

We have talked about various elements of store atmosphere, such as music, color, and scents. Now, you might ask, "Which element is the most important?" Well, the real secret to a great atmosphere lies in how different elements are combined. The magic word, therefore, is "congruence."

Congruence can be classified into three types:

1. *Atmospheric elements have to match the promoted product.* When deciding to use scents to create an appealing store atmosphere, congruence plays an important role. For example, if a chocolate specialty retailer intends to create pleasant surroundings in his store, it makes sense to use a chocolate scent. Likewise, florists can support their flower arrangements by using a flower scent. Many customers appreciate a pleasant scent in the air that matches the offered service or product. Indeed, the variety-seeking behavior of customers can

be enhanced when congruent scents are used.[58] Furthermore, congruent scents seem to influence consumers' moods positively: Fewer customers in a congruently scented setting reported being in a bad mood than those in an unscented setting.[59]

2. *Atmospheric elements have to be matched well with each other.* Scents and all other elements of store atmosphere (music, lighting, color) should not only match the products but also coordinate well with each other. Elements of the setting have to act together to provide an overall coherent atmosphere. This combination of matching elements in a store atmosphere leads to desirable consumer behavior. For example, the use of music and scents that match each other in terms of arousing qualities will positively influence impulse buying, customer satisfaction with the shopping experience, and even approach behavior.[60]

   For example, for creating a low-level arousing atmosphere, you could use scents like lavender and slow-tempo, soft music. Color should always be considered in combination with light. Light has a great impact on color perceptions. If you use soft light and dark colors, you can convey a prestigious image in your store. In contrast, bright fluorescent lights and warm colors will result in a discount image.[61]

3. *Atmospherics have to match the overall store concept.* Elements of a store's atmosphere should coordinate not only with each other and with the products presented but also with the overall store concept. For example, specialty stores targeting young, urban consumers could use pleasant but unconventional scents and rap music to attract their clientele.[62] Beside the target group, shopping motivation should also be considered. Does the store offer more task-oriented or hedonic products? Going to the supermarket to buy food will have a lower hedonic character than shopping for clothes (at least for most of us). It is much easier to use store atmosphere to create appealing feelings in a store environment patronized for recreational purposes (hedonic) than in task-oriented environments, where consumers are not very receptive to environmental cues.[63]

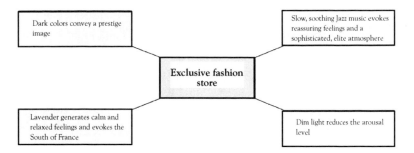

Figure 5.9. Matching store atmosphere elements in an exclusive fashion store.

Figure 5.9 provides an example of how the different elements of store atmosphere can be matched and coordinated to create the right atmosphere for an exclusive fashion store.

Takeaway Points

Here are the most important takeaway points from this chapter:

- Store atmosphere can be used to evoke pleasant moods. Happy customers spend more money, stay longer in the store, and are more satisfied with their shopping experience.
- Each environmental stimulus can be classified by its arousal and its pleasure level. Arousal refers to feelings of excitement and being stimulated, while pleasure describes enjoyable feelings. A store should aim at being pleasurable and achieving an optimal arousal level.
- Slow music can reduce the arousal level and keep shoppers longer in the store; fast, loud music evokes feelings of excitement and stimulation (but can also reduce the amount of time shoppers spend in a store).
- A unique, pleasant scent can effectively differentiate your store from the competition.
- Optimal ambient scents should not only be pleasant but also fit your store type.
- Light can be used to draw attention to products, to influence customers' level of arousal, and to help shoppers achieve

positive orientation in the store. In general, an increased level of illumination leads to more product contacts and more impulse purchases.

- Colors need must match the overall store image: Red alerts and attracts customers, while green and blue relaxes them. When choosing colors for a store, consider both their culture-bound symbolic meanings and the biological reactions they evoke in shoppers.
- Avoid crowding at all costs by using appropriate store design techniques.
- The most positive effects on shopping behavior can be achieved by congruent stimuli—that is, when all stimuli match each other, the merchandise, and the overall store concept well.

CHAPTER 6

Experiential Store Design
Make Shopping Memorable and Fun

Let's start this chapter inside a huge store, much larger than any other store you have ever seen. This store offers over 400 million different products. Books, movies, computers, electronics, toys, tools, furniture, jewelry—you name it, they most likely carry it. This store not only offers an enormous range of products but also is open 24 hours a day, 365 days a year. Further, the prices of most of the products in this store are very competitive, parking is never a problem, and shoppers receive personalized product suggestions based on their previous purchases. If that's not enough, many of the other shoppers in the store are more than willing to help you choose the items you need by pointing out their pros and cons. Would you like to compete with this store? Well, its name is Amazon.com. Like Amazon.com, there are many other online retailers on the Internet today. They all pose a serious challenge to brick-and-mortar stores.

In order to compete with online retailers, brick-and-mortar stores have to focus on their key advantages and emphasize what they do best:

- Some retailers, such as convenience stores, are located close to their customers.
- Other stores offer a very high level of personalized service that cannot be matched by online retailers.
- Still other brick-and-mortar stores thrive based on their connections with the local community.

There is another unique chance for retailers in this market. It is hard for online stores to match this strategy, and it can also give your store an edge over other traditional retail stores. We are talking about experiential store design.

Experiential marketing is all about creating unique, memorable experiences for consumers, and experiential store design has become an integral part of experiential marketing. More and more retailers realize today that they need to actively manage the customer experience in the store, and store design can play an important role in such experience management.[1] Customer experience management encompasses all the possible contact points a customer has with the company: advertising, special events, packaging, customer service phone attendants, the company Web site, and of course, the store or service facility itself.[2] Store design is only one such contact point. Even within the store, there are other factors, such as sales staff, that are important for creating a memorable, engaging customer experience. Nevertheless, store design does play a fundamental, irreplaceable role in experience creation due to the immediacy of the store environment. Whereas the recipient of advertising is a passive bystander, and even the user of a Web site cannot physically enter cyberspace, a shopper is surrounded by a three-dimensional, real-world store environment, which can be seen, touched, smelled, heard, and perhaps even tasted. It is these direct sensory impressions that make customer shopping experiences come alive.

Creating Unique Shopping Experiences

We have already seen how such atmospheric factors as music, colors, or scents and their direct influence on shopper behavior influence shoppers' moods and emotions. For example, happy music, when appropriate for the store, can considerably improve shoppers' moods. Designing a retail store in the right colors, such as blue, can have a relaxing effect on shoppers and encourage browsing.[3] While using appropriate emotional stimuli is clearly beneficial to retailers, experiential store design goes beyond this point. Its goal is to use a variety of emotional and cognitive stimuli to create a unique shopping experience for each customer. For example, the upscale department store Nordstrom doesn't simply play enjoyable music. Most stores feature a grand piano at a central location, and at select times, an elegantly dressed pianist entertains shoppers, bringing an extra touch of class to the store. While background music is probably played in every department store, listening to that same music played on an elegant grand piano is a unique Nordstrom experience (see Figure 6.1).

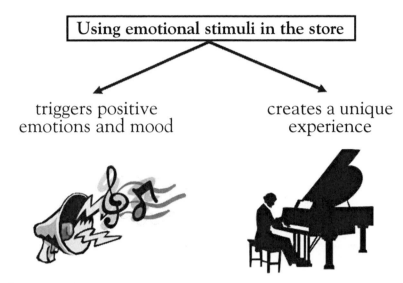

Using emotional stimuli in the store

triggers positive
emotions and mood

creates a unique
experience

Figure 6.1. Triggering just positive emotions versus creating a unique experience.

Today's consumers don't just shop to acquire products. They also want to have fun while they are shopping. This phenomenon is called "hedonic shopping" by consumer researchers and retail experts. Of course, not all shopping is hedonic in nature. If you run out of syrup for your morning waffles and quickly stop at the convenience store on your way home, you probably don't expect to be amused and entertained in that store. Instead, your shopping will be rational and task related, a clear case of utilitarian shopping.[4] Nevertheless, frequently consumers also expect fun, entertainment, fantasy, and amusement as part of shopping (see Figure 6.2).[5] This expectation can be a great chance for retailers. Creating stores that cater to the hedonic shopping motives of today's consumers can set some retailers apart from both their traditional and their online competitors. Furthermore, hedonic shopping motives increase both purchases and time spent in the store.[6]

Not all hedonic shopping is alike. There are actually six types of hedonic shopping motives:[7]

1. Adventure shopping
2. Social shopping
3. Gratification shopping

Figure 6.2. While some stores are designed for utilitarian shopping, others try to appeal to hedonic shoppers.

4. Idea shopping

5. Role shopping

6. Value shopping

These hedonic shopping motives are of course not mutually exclusive. A hedonic shopper may enjoy lunch in a jungle-themed restaurant, such as the Rainforest Café (adventure shopping), have a good time selecting birthday gifts for her grandchildren (role shopping), and get a kick out of finding a fashionable scarf for herself at a rock-bottom price (value shopping). And our research shows that it is not just women that engage in hedonic shopping. While there are gender differences with respect to which products men and women typically enjoy shopping for (think fashion accessories vs. consumer electronics), men can be just as captivated by unique shopping experiences as women can.

Let's take a closer look at the different types of hedonic shoppers and how store design can be used to create unique experiences for each of these very different shopper types.

Adventure Shoppers

Adventure shoppers desire stimulation while shopping. They want to enter a special place with a variety of exciting stimuli. Adventure shoppers are perhaps the type of hedonic shoppers most recognized by retailers and service business, judging by the number of companies that have, over the last decade, tried to appeal to them. Experiential marketing gurus Pine & Gilmore have identified four experience realms, three of which are suitable for adventure shoppers: aesthetic, entertainment, and escapist.[8]

Aesthetic experiences rely heavily on the elaborate design of the retail or service environment. Examples include the following:

- M&M World stores are dedicated to all things M&M. They are located in major tourist destinations like Orlando, Las Vegas, New York, and London. Visitors are almost overwhelmed by the many sensory impressions in these stores. A strong chocolate scent fills the air. One wall of the stores displays huge tubes filled with every possible color and variety of M&M chocolate candies. Oversized M&M characters can be seen running through the store. If you are unsure which M&M color is your favorite, try the M&M color mood analyzer. It will analyze which color best suits your current mood.
- Dark Room is a fashion store located in West London. It lives up to its name by displaying its eclectic fashion and housewares on pitch-black walls. The light focuses on the products only, thereby creating a sense of drama and excitement.
- Resort hotels and casinos in Las Vegas allow visitors to experience the Eiffel Tower, the Egyptian pyramids, and Venice's St. Mark's Square all in 1 day, thanks to elaborate theming. The granddaddy of all themed malls is also located in Las Vegas. At The Forum Shops, shoppers can experience what life in ancient Rome might have looked like had Rome been built by casino owners.
- Even car dealerships come up with new ways to dazzle their customers. According to press reports, a car dealership in Albany, New York, "turned a car wash into a hangar-sized mini amusement park and bazaar, featuring a diner, an Indonesian restaurant, a car-kitsch boutique, and a manicurist."[9]

Aesthetic experiences are frequently themed. This important design strategy is further discussed later in this chapter.

Entertaining experiences rely less on the store environment and more on the people (such as the sales staff or professional entertainers). Store design can, however, facilitate entertaining activities and provide a festive, fun, elegant, or carefree setting for them. Examples include the following:

- Exclusive fashion stores frequently stage seasonal fashion shows.
- Celebrity personal appearances generate excitement and increase store traffic.
- Stores provide live entertainment for their customers, such as magicians, origami artists, psychic readers, or caricaturists.
- Retailers feature live music in the store, either on a regular schedule or on special occasions.
- Many forms of entertainment are attached to holidays and seasonal events, such as Valentine's Day, Presidents' Day, the Chinese New Year, the Super Bowl, or even Elvis Presley's birthday.[10]

Escapist experiences are probably the most immersive and engaging of all adventure shopping approaches.

A perfect escapist experience was provided to visitors of the Adventurers Club, a nightclub on Pleasure Island at Walt Disney World in Orlando, Florida. The Adventurers Club represented a colonial club for world travelers. Its wood-paneled walls, library, statues, and assorted knickknacks transported guests back into the idealized British colonies of the early 1900s. However, what set the Adventurers club apart from many other themed attractions was the interactivity of the experience. Upon entering the club, guests were individually greeted (and gently mocked) by talking masks on the wall. While in the library, treasure room, or main salon, the regular club members, eccentric characters like club president Pamela Perkins or aviator Hathaway Brown, mingled with the guests and often chatted with them at length about subjects like aviation or bugs. The club even had its own rituals and traditions, like the official greeting (Kungaloosh!), the club salute, and a club theme song. The Adventurers Club closed in 2009 due to a restructuring of the Pleasure Island district. However, escapist experiences can still be found at other venues nearby:

- Not far from Pleasure Island, Disney's competitor, Universal, recently opened a Harry Potter theme park. At the core of The Wizarding World of Harry Potter is a truly escapist shopping center themed to be the magical village of Hogsmeade. There, Harry Potter fans big and small can buy items, such as magic wands (true to the J. K. Rowling book, the shopper doesn't select the wand, but the wand selects the shopper), and feast on butter beer, a drink described in the Harry Potter books but especially brewed for the park.

- Another prime example of a retailer creating an escapist experience is American Girl doll stores. In these stores in several American cities, young girls and their mothers can have the ultimate doll experience (see Figure 6.3). The expansive stores feature a doll boutique, a hairdressing salon for dolls, a theater, party rooms, a doll hospital, and even a restaurant where dolls in miniature chairs sit at the table with their owners and "eat" from doll-sized plates.[11]

- A very different group of shoppers will experience an escapist adventure at Mark's Work Wearhouse. Shoppers who want to test how warm the winter wear they are buying really is can try it on in a walk-in freezer. The freezer, which usually runs at balmy 60°F, can at the request of more adventurous shoppers

Figure 6.3. A young shopper having the ultimate doll experience at an American Girl store.

be turned down all the way to a brutal –40°F. In addition, the shop features several other interactive displays, including surfaces, such as roof shingles and concrete, to test shoes.[12]

Social Shoppers

Social shoppers see shopping as an occasion for social interaction. They enjoy shopping together with family members or friends and may also enjoy talking to sales staff and other shoppers. To focus on the needs of social shoppers, retailers need to create environments that facilitate social interaction. One thing they can do is create so-called third places. The term "third place" was coined by sociologist Ray Oldenburg. In his book *The Great Good Place*, he deplores the lack of informal meeting places in today's society:

> The examples set by societies that have solved the problem of place and those set by small towns and vital neighborhoods of our past suggest that daily life, in order to be relaxed and fulfilling must find its balance in three realms of experience. One is domestic, a second is gainful or productive, and the third is inclusively sociable, offering both the basis of community and the celebration of it . . . In the newer American communities, third places are neither prominent nor prolific. Upon an urban landscape increasingly hostile to and devoid of informal gathering places, one may encounter people rather pathetically trying to find some spot in which to relax and enjoy each other's company.[13]

According to Oldenburg, third places are low-key, informal meeting places where people can gather. The concept of the third place has been successfully implemented by Starbucks. The company carefully designs its stores to convey a comfortable, relaxing, and slightly upscale atmosphere that encourages patrons to linger and communicate.[14] While Starbucks cafés explicitly specialize in being third places, the concept of the third place can be incorporated successfully in other settings:

- Shopping malls provide shoppers with comfortable areas where they can meet and relax before heading to the mall stores again (see Figure 6.4).

Figure 6.4. The mall as a third place.

- Both malls and large stores feature designated meeting points that help families or other groups of shoppers find each other.
- Playgrounds in malls and stores provide opportunities for both children and parents to meet and interact with other shoppers.
- Bookstores, such as Barnes & Noble and Borders, invariably include cafés. In many communities, these stores have become places for high school students to collectively do their homework, retired people to meet over coffee, and young single adults to flirt and meet others their own age (see Figure 6.5).

To appeal to social shoppers, retailers need to consider the family members or friends who accompany the shopper and to cater to their needs as well. In general, research shows that people shopping with companions visit more areas in a store and also purchase more.[15] However, there are also shopping situations where companions, in particular family members, can deteriorate the experience of the shopper.[16] In this case, retailers need to take action and implement store design techniques that can help. This solution is exemplified by an in-store observation we carried out for one of our clients. In fashion stores, we found that female shoppers were more likely to purchase clothes they tried on in the fitting room when their male companions were provided a comfortable chair

Figure 6.5. Bookstores created in-store cafes and relaxation zones for shoppers to relax, do homework, meet other people, and even read books.

to sit in as well as gender-specific reading material while they waited for their wives or girlfriends. Comfort and entertainment kept the guys happy, which in turn translated into a more relaxed shopping experience for the women. Retailers can even display selected male accessories, such as ties, close to the female fitting rooms. This could lead to two positive effects at once. Social shoppers who are less interrupted by their companions will stay in a shopping mood longer, and retailers may even generate additional income by encouraging the shopping companions to make unplanned purchases.

Gratification Shoppers

Gratification shoppers shop to treat themselves to something special. This kind of shopping is often done to relax, relieve stress after a difficult day at work, or get in a better mood. Gratification shoppers engage in an activity that is sometimes jokingly referred to as "retail therapy." The key to reaching gratification shoppers is to create opportunities for relaxation, pampering, and—most importantly—*instant* gratification. Examples related to store design and visual merchandising include the following:

- Retailers can provide facilities for relaxation and pampering. These can range from simple measures, such as placing massage chairs in the store (like the ones found in every Brookstone), to free makeup stations in the cosmetic department of many department stores, all the way to elaborate in-store spas.
- Product sampling can serve as antecedent stimuli, promising forthcoming gratification and triggering impulse purchases in gratification shoppers.
- Merchandising techniques that use the scarcity principle to increase the exclusivity of the merchandise—such as displaying only a very few pieces of each product—can enhance the product's value to gratification shoppers.
- Whenever possible, barriers to instant gratification, such as locked-away products or over-the-counter service, should be removed. Obviously, this technique needs to be counterbalanced with the necessity to prevent shoplifting as well as the legal requirements of certain products.

Idea Shoppers

Idea shoppers use shopping trips as occasions to learn about new products, services, fashions, or technological trends. As pollster Mark Penn points out, 78% of American consumers say that advertising doesn't provide them with enough of the information they need. They often fill in the gaps with online research. As Penn further notes, 24% of shoppers even do research before they buy shampoo.[17] In spite of the important role of the Internet today, idea shoppers also enjoy browsing for information in brick-and-mortar stores.

The idea shopper's pleasure in browsing can be enhanced by providing ample information about products. The key is to provide plenty of information for those idea shoppers who seek it, yet not overwhelm the average shopper who may be confused or annoyed by too much (technical) product information. A possible solution can be found in some electronics and office stores. Next to the complex products (e.g., computers, cameras, and office machines), laminated cards are attached to the store fixtures. On the front, these cards provide basic product information desired by most shoppers. When flipped over, though, the cards reveal much more detailed information (usually in smaller print) desired by idea shoppers.

Technology can also be used to satisfy the information requirements of idea shoppers: Target has developed an app for the iPhone that provides shoppers with additional information on the products they see in the store. The shopper can scan the product's bar code by taking a picture of it and is immediately provided with detailed product information.

Role Shoppers

Role shoppers enjoy the act of buying gifts for the people they love. Occasions for gift shopping are major holidays, such as Christmas, Hanukkah, the end of Ramadan, and Valentine's Day, as well as more personal occasions, such as birthdays, anniversaries, weddings, graduations, or the birth of a child. For some people, even divorce parties have become occasions for gift giving[18] (whatever an appropriate gift for that occasion might be). The following are some ideas for how retailers can better appeal to role shoppers:

- Seasonal decorations can induce the gift shopper's shopping motivation. For example, at Christmas a multisensory "Christmas World" in the store (consisting of Christmas symbols, colors, and scents) can reinforce the idea of gift buying.
- Seasonal store signs can subtly remind shoppers of their social obligations on appropriate occasions, such as Mother's Day or Valentine's Day. Pictures can be used for their superiority for conveying emotional messages. For example, on Valentine's Day, pictures can show a good husband what he can buy for his wife.
- In large stores, a specialized gift department can increase the convenience of shopping for gifts. A gift-wrapping service can make gift shopping even more convenient and enjoyable for some role shoppers.
- Experiences can be pleasurable not only for gift givers but also for those they present their gifts to. These manufactured experiences—which appeal to gratification shoppers—range from skydiving, country hotel weekends, personal shopping

days, and stays at a health spa all the way to the odd and peculiar experiences (e.g., walking with wolves, swimming with dolphins, or bungee jumping).[19]

Finally, gift shoppers are not just an important target group for retailers. As research has shown, consumers who shop for others are also happier than those who only shop for themselves.[20] Committed role shoppers seem to have known this truth for a long time. It's now up to retailers to spread that good news to other shoppers.

Value Shoppers

Value shoppers are essentially bargain hunters. These deal-prone consumers enjoy bargains and discounts. It should be pointed out that it is not simply the low price they are after. (Utilitarian shoppers value low prices, too.) It is also the thrill of bargain hunting and the sense of personal achievement they gain from it.

Retailers that cater specifically to value shoppers (in addition to price-conscious utilitarian shoppers) are dollar stores such as Dollar General or Dollar Tree. Pop-up stores are a more recent concept. These are retail stores that arrive unannounced in empty storefronts and close their doors again after a temporary stay, which can range from a weekend to a few weeks. Their goal is to take shoppers by surprise.[21] Because of the transient nature of these stores, they appeal to value shoppers who enjoy discovering them and shopping in them for as long as they last.

Mainstream retailers can, however, learn how to appeal to value shoppers as well:

- Specific parts of a store can be dedicated to bargain hunters. In department stores, this is often the bargain basement.
- Product displays can also signal bargains—and a challenge to be conquered—for value shoppers. Love them or hate them, bargain bins with piles of merchandise to sift through provide bargain hunters with the challenge they crave.
- Similarly, bazaar-like shopping environments (which may, of course, be purposefully built in that way) can also provide value shoppers with the thrill of the bargain hunt.

- The color scheme of the store or the merchandise display can signal to value shoppers that there is a deal to be made. In numerous countries ranging from the United States to Thailand, we have observed that retailers use the color combination yellow-red to signal low prices, clearance sales, and special bargains.

With all the tools and techniques we have discussed, however, care must be taken to never negatively impact the overall price and quality perception of the store. A "cheap" color combination or a row of bargain bins may attract bargain shoppers, but at the same time, these can have unintended consequences for the positioning of the store. The name of the game is separation. Bargain basements (far away from the regularly priced merchandise), outlet centers in the desert, and bargain areas discreetly hidden in the back of a store all serve this purpose for upscale retailers.

Creating a Memorable Experience

To create engaging, memorable experiences for hedonic shoppers, careful planning is required. After all, simply combining colors, music, scents, textures, and lights won't guarantee success. Experiential retailers are advised to take the following four steps.[22]

1. *Collect a variety of different ideas for creating a memorable experience.* Creativity techniques, such as brainstorming or mind maps, can be used to create new ideas. When brainstorming for possible unique customer experiences, retailers can refer to the following:

- The merchandise sold
- Cultural trends
- The company's history
- The target audience

The focus should be on unique, memorable experiences that cannot easily be imitated by the competition. A collection of possible starting points for the creation of experiences can be seen in Table 6.1.

Table 6.1. Starting Points for the Development of Unique Experiences

Achievement	Humor
Affluence	Indulgence
Athleticism	Knowledge
Celebrity	Meditation
Comfort	Nature
Eroticism	Nostalgia
Exoticism	Prestige
Exuberance	Sociability
Fantasy	Success
Freedom	Surprise
Health	Technology

Sources: Kroeber-Riel, Weinberg, and Groeppel-Klein (2009).

2. *Eliminate unsuitable experiences.* Ask the following question to eliminate unsuitable experiences:

- Does the experience relate to the values of the target group?
- Does the experience fit in with long-term trends rather than temporary fads?
- Does the experience carry any negative associations?
- Does the experience fit the company's corporate identity?
- Can the experience be easily copied by the competition?
- How unique is the experience?
- Does the company have the resources and capabilities to implement the experience well?

3. *Develop and test your experience concept.* At this stage, marketing research comes into the mix. Before consumers can provide input about what they like or dislike about a chosen experience, a concept needs to be developed. This concept can be a verbal description of the experience, drawings, three-dimensional models, or preferably a combination of all of these techniques. The concept is then tested by requesting feedback from an appropriate group of target consumers, most commonly in the form of qualitative research, such as focus groups where participants are presented with the concept and asked to comment on it.

4. *Implement the chosen experience.* Only when the experience concept is in place should the implementation or design of the experience actually begin.

Staging a Believable Experience

"All the world's a stage, and all the men and women merely players," Jaques declares in Shakespeare's *As You Like It.*[23] This theatrical metaphor was also picked by sociologist Erving Goffman to analyze the social interactions between people as if they were part of a theatrical performance.[24] Indeed, retail and service businesses can be compared to theatrical productions, and the dramaturgical perspective of a stage presentation can provide valuable insights to experiential marketers.

A central tenant of Goffman's dramaturgical perspective is that the goal of a theatrical production is to stage a performance believable for the audience. This goal can only be achieved if all aspects of the theater work together perfectly—the actors, the stage, and the props, to name just a few. When staging an experience for shoppers, a believable performance is also essential. To achieve this outcome, all aspects of the retail show (to which we refer to here with their theatrical terms) must fall into place easily and well.

Script

To stage a great show, a great script is essential. In the case of experiential retailing, the script is the company's overall strategy, which also includes a long-term, strategic approach to creating and staging experiences.

Actors

In a theater performance, the actors must be carefully selected (casting). They must rehearse their roles, wear the appropriate costumes for their roles, stick to their scripts, and at all times work together with other members of the cast to make the performance credible to the audience. Applied to a retail setting, a credible experience for customers can only be achieved with the right staff.

In the context of this book, we deal primarily with the physical environment of the performance. However, engaging, memorable experiences rely largely on having the right staff. In some experiential stores, the emphasis may be on store design (such as in the aesthetic experiences described already), but even in these settings staff remains essential. Retailers who try to stage more immersive experiences must rely even more on their frontline personnel. On stage, untalented or unenthusiastic actors will ruin every show, even those with a good script and the help of other fine actors. Likewise, in experiential retailing, incompetent, poorly trained, or cold salespeople can never be counterweighted by store design and visual merchandising, no matter how dazzling the store may look. Even the most experienced experiential marketers will at times have problems with the quality of their cast: When The Walt Disney Corporation opened its first theme park on European soil, Euro Disney in Paris, France (since rebranded as Disneyland Paris), it was difficult to recruit and train staff that was motivated to convey the "Disney magic" of a fun and friendly family experience delivered with a smile. As one French staff member famously said, "I'll smile if I want to. Convince me."[25]

Stage

The stage in a theater is divided into the front stage and the back stage. The front stage is where the actors perform. It is visible to the audience. Everything on the front stage must be designed to create a believable show. It is the responsibility of scenic designers to create the perfect setting in which the actors can act. If the scenery is of poor quality, the play will suffer. The back stage, while not visible to the audience, is equally important for a believable show. On the back stage, the actors practice their roles, they wait until they are called to the stage, and they relax in between performances. You can easily transfer this dramaturgical metaphor to the retail store: In a store, the front stage is the sales floor, and in a restaurant, it is the dining room. It is the physical environment that customers can see and, indeed, the focus of this book.

Every detail on the front stage must be carefully planned and orchestrated. Imagine a play set in the 1800s where the salon on stage looks like a 1970s living room? How believable would that be? Even if only one piece of furniture on that stage looks like it was from the 1970s, it can ruin the show. Similarly, in the store, every single detail of the store design must fit. For example, if a cosmetics store is designed to convey an experience in nature, store fixtures and merchandise displays made of plastic might ruin the shoppers' experience, even if the store is otherwise lavishly themed with trees, grass, flowers, and other nature-related items.

Just like the back stage in a theater, storage rooms, offices, and break rooms for the sales staff are not visible to the shoppers (the audience). Nevertheless, they contribute to a believable show out on the sales floor (the front stage). For instance, the layout and location of storage rooms must be designed to facilitate delivery of the merchandise to the sales floor. If this is not the case, the shopping experience can be severely impacted. It is for this reason that cold-storage rooms in supermarkets are frequently located next to the dairy department, so that shelves can easily be refilled through openings in the wall without ever disturbing shoppers.

Theater people know that the entrance to the back stage must be guarded at all times. If members of the audience were able to enter the back stage, they would see the actors in a completely different way and the theater's image would be broken. On the back stage, the actors don't play their roles, they don't follow the script, and they may not even wear their costumes. One of the authors once participated in a TV talk show hosted by a former singer, a middle-aged woman renowned for her grace and style. Seeing her in the green room (backstage) an hour before the start of the show without makeup, wearing old jeans, and humming a song clearly not meant for public consumption was endearing, but it was also clear that she would never want and, indeed, would never let her audience see her that way.

In a retail store or service business, the entrance to the back stage must also be protected at all times. Otherwise the audience's experience may be ruined. In a restaurant, if the door to the kitchen is left open, guests see an environment quite different from the dining room. The efficient layout and sterile-looking appliances and the bustling of chefs, waitstaff, and kitchen helpers provide a stark contrast to the elegant design of the dining room. Even if the staff carefully follows all instructions related to hygiene, the kitchen may look disorderly or even chaotic in the eyes of the guest.[26] Likewise, a shopper who catches a glimpse of the minimalist storage room of a lavishly designed flagship store may have her overall shopping experience be negatively impacted.

While in a theater, the front stage and the auditorium are separated; in a retail store, the shoppers are directly on the front stage. Therefore, it is necessary to ensure that the back stage does not encroach on the front stage, such as cleaning supplies left in the store, personal items of the sales staff on display for all customers to see, and so on. Finally, on occasion, stores may open (part of) the back stage to customers, as this can be a memorable experience by itself. Examples of this tactic include the following:

- Restaurant kitchens where the food is prepared in front of the guests (e.g., in some Japanese restaurants)
- Backstage tours, as offered by the Disney and Universal theme parks
- Art shops where artists create objects on the sales floor in front of the shoppers, such as in glassblowing shops in Venice

Such staged glimpses behind the scenes can also constitute enjoyable and memorable experiences for shoppers and serve as a point of differentiation for stores. Retailers just need to make sure that the shoppers never stumble onto the real back stage (where many of the Venetian glassblowing shops keep the Chinese imports).

Theming Your Store

Sometimes people wish that they were in a different place or could visit a different time period. How about exploring the Amazon rain forest, walking through a haunted Scottish castle, having dinner on an undersea coral reef, or buying Marie Antoinette's finest china in Versailles? Consumers can do all these things without the time required for overseas travel, the worries of catching a cold in a damp and poorly ventilated medieval building, the expense and fatigue of diving lessons, or the peril of being beheaded by the zealots from the French Revolution. The architectural-theatrical method that allows all these escapists to experience their favorite adventures is called theming.

Theming is an important experiential marketing technique employed by many (though not all) stores, malls, and service businesses discussed in this chapter. In themed environments, most of the elements are designed to tell a story in which the visitor plays a part.[27] The physical attributes of the environment (layout, color, architecture), all emotional and cognitive stimuli (sound, scents, light textures), the staff (costumes, makeup), and the products sold should be part of the theme.[28] Through theming, exciting, out-of-the-ordinary artificial worlds are created in which consumers participate.[29] Theming gives the institution or place a precise, unique meaning, differentiates it from the competition, and thus make it more attractive and interesting in the eyes of the consumer.[30]

Because of these benefits, many examples of themed environments exist in the service industry, including the following:

- Theme parks (e.g., Walt Disney World, the world's largest theme park and themed resort)
- Hotels (e.g., the famous Madonna Inn in San Luis Obispo, California, where guests can sleep in a variety of opulently themed rooms, including the famous caveman room)
- Restaurants (e.g., Bubba Gump Shrimp Co. restaurants, inspired by the movie *Forrest Gump*)
- Casinos (e.g., virtually all casinos in Las Vegas: Circus Circus, Luxor, and Treasure Island, to name a few)
- Zoos (e.g., Animal Kingdom, a hybrid between a zoo and a theme park, which is part of Walt Disney World)
- Museums (e.g., the Museum of Immigration on Ellis Island, New York, where visitors can relive the experience of immigrants arriving in New York Harbor at the turn of the 20th century)
- Aquariums (e.g., the Acquario di Genova in Genoa, Italy, where visitors feel like they are in the middle of an ocean)
- Towns (e.g., Colonial Williamsburg, Virginia, an entire colonial town recreated for visitors to experience)

In restaurants, theming has become so prevalent that it has even attracted the attention of humorists. For example, in 1998 a tongue-in-cheek article on the satirist Web site *The Onion* stated that the "Nation's Last Themeless Restaurant Closes":

DUBUQUE, IA—An era came to an end Tuesday when Pat's Place, the nation's last themeless restaurant, closed its doors in

Dubuque. "We achieved a certain local notoriety for our unique non-themed food and unadorned atmosphere," said owner Patrick Baines, "but sales were sluggish, as most people would just come in to gawk at our photoless walls and mundanely named menu items like 'hamburger' and 'pancakes.' Then they would head over to the Rainforest Cafe, Hard Rock Cafe, Planet Hollywood, All-Star Cafe, Johnny Rocket's or Disney Cafe down the street." Once vacated by Baines, the building will become home to Dubuque's seventh Paddy O'Touchdown's Irish Sports Bar & Good-Tyme Internet Grill.[31]

In retailing, both individual stores and entire shopping malls can be themed. While any type of store can be themed (such as Jungle Jim's supermarket in Cincinnati or Necromance, a rather creepy, death-themed gift store in Los Angeles), theming is particularly popular in flagship stores, such as those for Apple, Prada, Nike, or Nokia.

Themed malls have also become very popular. Famous examples, in addition to the already mentioned Forum Shops in Las Vegas, include the gigantic West Edmonton Mall in Canada and the Ibn Battuta Mall in Dubai. The West Edmonton Mall includes several themed areas, including Chinatown, a New Orleans–inspired area and a "Europa Boulevard." The Ibn Battuta Mall is named after the Arab explorer Ibn Battuta, and the various areas of the mall are lavishly themed to represent the far corners of the world visited by this adventurer: India, China, Persia, Egypt, Tunisia, and Andalusia.

While theming can help attract customers and differentiate a company from its competition, not all attempts at theming are successful, as exemplified by a chain of nautically themed restaurants named "Dive!" The chain, partly owned by Stephen Spielberg, created a considerable amount of media attention. While the theming was ingenious—both inside and outside, the restaurants looked like submarines—they were never financially successful. After only 5 years, the company took a nosedive and the restaurants closed.[32] The reasons for such failures of themed business are numerous:

- Theming can be a capital-intensive endeavor and may ultimately prove too costly.

- The chosen theme may not appeal to the target group.
- The frontline personnel may not be appropriately trained or motivated to fulfill their role in the theme.[33]

In order to be successful, theming must be done right. Valuable advice is given by Marty Sklar, former president of "imagineering" at the Walt Disney Company, who oversaw the construction of several of the company's theme parks. He expresses his advice as "Mickey's 10 Commandments":

1. Know your audience—Don't bore people, talk down to them, or lose them by assuming that they know what you know.
2. Wear your guest's shoes—Insist that designers, staff, and your board members experience your facility as visitors as often as possible.
3. Organize the flow of people and ideas—Use good story-telling techniques, tell good stories not lectures, and lay out your exhibit with a clear logic.
4. Create a weenie—Lead visitors from one area to another by creating visual magnets and giving visitors rewards for making the journey
5. Communicate with visual literacy—Make good use of all the non-verbal ways of communication—color, shape, form, texture.
6. Avoid overload—Resist the temptation to tell too much, to have too many objects; don't force people to swallow more than they can digest; try to stimulate and provide guidance to those who want more.
7. Tell one story at a time—If you have a lot of information, divide it into distinct, logical, organized stories; people can absorb and retain information more clearly if the path to the next concept is clear and logical.
8. Avoid contradiction—Clear institutional identity helps give you the competitive edge. The public needs to know who you are and what differentiates you from other institutions they may have seen.
9. For every ounce of treatment, provide a ton of fun—How do you woo people away from all other temptations? Give people plenty of opportunity to enjoy themselves by emphasizing ways that let people participate in the experience and making your environment rich and appealing to all senses.

10. Keep it up—Never underestimate the importance of cleanliness and routine maintenance; people expect to get a good show every time; people will comment more on broken and dirty stuff.[34]

While many factors contribute to successful theming, some are particularly important. We call them the 4 As of successful theming:

1. Appropriate theme
2. Attention to detail
3. Authenticity
4. Attitude of the staff

Choosing an Appropriate Theme

Should your store look like a jungle, a Victorian boutique, or Star Trek's USS *Enterprise*? Themes can be drawn from many sources. They can reflect the physical world, religion, politics and history, fashion and popular culture, the arts, and even philosophical and psychological concepts.[35] Possible sources for themes, as well as examples of them, can be found in Table 6.2.

When selecting a theme, the values and preference of the target group must be closely considered.[36] For example, in a survey we conducted among European consumers, we found that, in general, the themes "tropical paradise," "Venice," and "classical civilization" were preferred. However, the results also indicated that there are considerable differences in the preferences of men and women, as well as for different age groups. Most importantly, the consumers preferred different themes for different stores and service businesses. For example, while they liked a tropical theme in hotels, travel agencies, and zoos, they found that theme much less suitable for fashion stores or supermarkets. For the latter, a futuristic theme was rated highest. These results are clearly place and time specific and should not be generalized, but the opinions do emphasize the importance of choosing the right theme for the right venture, a decision that should ideally be based on solid empirical data.

Table 6.2. Some Interesting Sources for Themes

Theme	Examples	
Tropical paradise	Polynesia, Florida, Hawaii, the Caribbean	Jungle Jim's, Cincinnati, Ohio
Status	Castles, palaces	Burj al Arab hotel (7-star hotel), Dubai
Wild West	Ghost town, saloon	The Wild Wild West store, Dallas, Texas
Classical civilization	Ancient Rome, ancient Greece, pharaonic Egypt	Forum Shops, Las Vegas
Nostalgia	Country store, Main Street USA	Cracker Barrel Old Country Store and Restaurant chain
Arabian fantasy	Arabian nights, Oriental bazaars, Morocco	The Casbah Fashion Store and Café, Los Angeles
Urban motif	New York, London, San Francisco	Ted Baker, Chicago
Exotic or romantic places	Venice, Paris, Bangkok	The Venetian, Las Vegas
Modernism and progress	Purist, clean lines, technology	Apple stores
Music	Rock, jazz, classical music	Hard Rock Cafe
Sports	Baseball, football, hockey, soccer	Niketown flagship stores
Hollywood and movies	Tinseltown, cartoons, Casablanca	Planet Hollywood
Iconic buildings	Eiffel Tower, the Sphinx	Luxor, Las Vegas
Fashion	Models, clothes	Victoria's Secret flagship store, New York
Literature	Harry Potter, Sherlock Holmes	Jekyll & Hyde Club, New York
Nature	The rain forest, the desert, volcanoes	Bass Pro Shops
Abstract concepts	Conservation, creation, religion	The Holy Land Experience, Orlando, Florida
The company itself	Flagship stores celebrating the company and its logo	M&M World, World of Coca-Cola

Sources: Based on Bryman (2004); Gottdiener (1997); Schmitt and Simonson (1997).

Attention to Detail

You have already learned about the dramaturgical perspective and how important it is to stage a believable performance. This is especially true when a shopping environment is themed. Attention must be given to even the smallest details; otherwise the illusion created by the theme will be destroyed—which will, in turn, lead to disappointment or even cynical reactions from the shoppers.

Authenticity

Another issue that designers, owners, and managers of themed stores or malls need to deal with is authenticity. For instance, how important is it that an American fashion store themed as a Parisian boutique uses genuine French furniture, decorations, and artwork? Some experts claim that consumers are searching for the "objectively authentic,"[37] whereas others contend that consumers are searching only for an enjoyable illusion.[38] Based on our research on theming, we take a somewhat different position. The decision of whether to use the fake versus authentic very much depends on the background of the shoppers. When the shoppers are familiar with the culture, historical period, place, or story on which the theme is based, stereotypical artifacts and symbols should be avoided. Instead, genuine artifacts should be used.

In the case of the Parisian-themed fashion store, if it is likely that the shoppers are familiar with French culture. In an upscale store located in Manhattan, authentic French artwork and furniture should be incorporated in the design of the store. On the other hand, shoppers who show little familiarity with the cultural background of the theme will be more satisfied when their stereotypical expectations are met.[39] This facet explains why both highly stereotypical theming, such as the Rainforest Café, and themed venues where historical buildings are incorporated in the theme, such as South Street Seaport in New York or Covent Garden in London, can be highly successful—they must cater to the right people in the right place and in the right manner.

The Attitude of the Staff

The physical environment of a store is obviously essential for the theme to work. But so is the staff. A customer-centered demeanor on the part of the sales staff is a success factor in both themed and nonthemed stores and service businesses. After all, what good does a carefully planned theme do if the waiter is rude or the salesclerk inattentive? In addition, the staff needs to be carefully trained and motivated to appropriately play their roles as part of the overarching theme. This focus includes the following:

1. Wearing the appropriate costumes for their roles. For example, the staff in a status-themed store must wear clothes that fit their role within the theme.
2. Using the right words and the right accent. In an Italian-themed store, the salespeople need to be able to correctly pronounce the Italian brands they sell (and, equally important, refrain from correcting the pronunciation of their customers).
3. Having the knowledge to play their part. In a high-tech themed store, the sales staff needs to be up to date with all the technology products they sell.

As in a theater or in a movie, in the end, it is the actors who get either the catcalls or the applause.

Takeaway Points

Here are the most important takeaway points from this chapter:

- Customer experiences need to be managed well, and store design can play an important role in customer experience management because of the direct, three-dimensional sensory impressions such design can provide.
- Experiential store design is more than just creating positive emotions—the aim is to create unique, memorable experiences for shoppers.
- Consumers shop for utilitarian and hedonic reasons. Hedonic shopping—shopping for pleasure and not out of necessity— has become increasingly important today. Marketers need to understand the varied hedonic shopping motives in order to create the right experiences for the right target groups.
- While many retailers use experiential store design to target adventure shoppers (which are indeed an important hedonic shopping segment), store design can also be used to attract

and impress other types of hedonic shoppers—social shoppers, gratification shoppers, idea shoppers, role shoppers, and value shoppers.

- To create memorable experiences, a marketer must take certain steps: (a) Collect ideas for experiences, (b) eliminate unsuitable experiences, (c) develop and test concepts for consumer reactions, and (d) implement the chosen experience well.
- To stage a believable performance, experiential marketers must look at their business as if it were a theater. By using the dramaturgical perspective, important insights are revealed as to what it takes to stage a good show.
- Theming can help differentiate a store from its competition and make it more attractive and interesting for shoppers—but only if theming is done right.
- To create good theming, follow "Mickey's 10 Commandments" and apply the 4 As of successful theming: appropriate theme, attention to detail, authenticity, and attitude of the staff.

CHAPTER 7

A Cookbook for Best Store Design

Seven Recipes

Sometimes you want quick fixes for specific problems in a store. This is what we try to give you in this chapter. Here we provide you with concise and practical recipes for how to influence shopping behavior through store design and visual merchandising. As with all good recipes, however, feel free to modify where useful, add additional creative ingredients, or discard the recipes altogether—we want our cookbook to suit your specific needs. Bon appétit!

Recipe 1: Shorten Wait-Time Perception

Do you hate waiting? Most consumers do (the authors included). In fact, shoppers frequently mention waiting as their most important complaint about retail stores.[1] Furthermore, waiting is an important factor in the decision of where to shop.[2] Unfortunately, given today's capacity constraints and labor costs, in most stores it is unrealistic to completely eliminate waiting at the checkout, the deli department, the customer service desk, or the fitting room. It is, however, possible to use store design to shorten perceived waiting time. This goal can be achieved by making the waiting experience both entertaining and equitable.

Perceived waiting time can be reduced by providing entertainment to divert the shoppers' attention from the wait. This principle is well known by the major theme parks. Walt Disney World in Orlando, Florida, has even built an underground operational command center where employees monitor waiting lines at the rides. When wait times get too long, they can instantly dispatch Disney characters or even a miniparade called "Move it! Shake it! Celebrate it!" to entertain the waiting crowds or attract them into less crowded parts of the theme park.[3] A more conventional example is seen in Figure 7.1. Monitors mounted over the checkout counter at a supermarket make waiting more palatable with presentation of news, cartoons, and even an occasional in-store commercial. One word of caution, though: Checkout areas are great places for buying impulse products. If the programs shown on the monitors are too attractive and interesting, shoppers will likely make fewer impulse purchases.

Waiting appears shorter when it is perceived as equitable.[4] In certain shopping situations, this equity can be achieved with a "take-a-ticket" system. For example, at a deli counter, a ticket dispenser is effective. Shoppers take sequentially numbered tickets as they arrive and are served when their ticket number is called. There is no cutting into the line under this system. What's more, this type of managed waiting is also seen as more comfortable because there is no need to stand in a line.

Maybe it is just us, but when we line up at a checkout, we invariably get the feeling that the other lines move faster, which seems unfair to the customer. There is a solution, though. Instead of parallel lines to multiple servers, a single line to multiple servers (also called a "snake" line)[5] can be implemented (Figure 7.2). This solves the problem of multiple lines moving at different speeds. In research we conducted, we

Figure 7.1. A monitor mounted over a checkout counter.

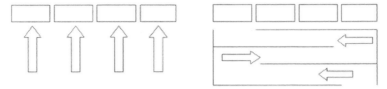

Figure 7.2. Different wait-line configurations: Multiple lines for multiple servers (left) and a single snake line (right).

found that consumers standing in a snake line felt that their waiting time was shorter compared to waiting in one of several parallel lines (even though objectively, of course, the wait time was on average the same). This illusion was due to the fact that customers considered waiting more fair and equitable in this different line configuration.[6]

Recipe 2: Alter Shoppers' Price Perceptions

Have you ever been in the clearance section of a T. J. Maxx store? In the clearance area of the housewares department, you will find seashells next to picture frames, DVDs on top of potpourri jars, scented candles, cookbooks, metal hooks, dog shampoo, and a box of Butter Almond Toffees, all on the same shelf. It all looks as if a minor tornado had just touched down on the clearance shelves. This topsy-turvy merchandise presentation may not be to everyone's liking, but it is done on purpose, and it certainly reinforces the low-price image of off-price retailers like T. J. Maxx, Ross, or Marshalls.

Store design and visual merchandising can influence shoppers' price perceptions. It can also work both ways: Products can be made to appear more affordable or alternatively more exclusive and expensive. It all depends on the context in which the merchandise is presented. If a retailer wishes to convey a low price, the following cues will lower price perceptions:

- Use of the color combination yellow and red, which shoppers have learned to associate with sales and discount stores
- A simple décor
- Signs that state both the sales price as well as a (lower) reference price ("Instead of $15 now only $7")
- Use of "broken" prices on price tags ($6.99 instead of $7; $29.95 instead of $30)
- Displaying a large quantity of each product

The latter technique is successfully used by some discount retailers as a power aisle. In a power aisle, large quantities of a relatively small number of stock-keeping units are displayed. This massed-out look has been shown to significantly lower the overall price perceptions of shoppers in the store.[7]

If, on the other hand, an exclusive, high-priced image is desired for a product, this goal can be achieved by using the following techniques:

- Placing a product among high-priced products will increase the perceived exclusiveness of that product.
- Presenting a product on a single pedestal or under a glass cover will also make the product appear to be more luxurious or exclusive.

Environmental cues can also make the whole store appear more upscale. Examples are the use of high-status music (classical music or jazz) as well as soft floors. It is important to make sure that all the cues are congruent because a single misplaced cue can destroy the image of luxury and exclusivity. In general, upscale retailers should follow the rule of "Less is more." The fewer products that are on display, the more exclusive that store will appear to customers.

Recipe 3: Cater to the Shopping Interests of Senior Citizens

Of all demographic trends influencing marketing today, the changing age structure of society is by far the most pervasive. Increased life expectancy (by itself a most gratifying trend), together with a low fertility rate, has had a significant impact on the composition of the population in most industrialized countries. As the baby boom generation grows older, in the United States the percentage of the population aged 65 and older will increase from 13% in 2010 to 19% in 2030.[8] In most Western European countries, that change will be even more pronounced.

Already there are over 40 million Americans aged 65 and older.[9] While this group constitutes a lucrative market for many marketers, senior citizens do have unique wants and interests that need to be addressed.

As people age, their bodies undergo biological changes. For example, visual acuity may decrease, colors are perceived somewhat differently, hearing may be impaired, and bone mass decreases steadily, to name just a few of these changes. Not all mature consumers experience these physical and sensory changes to the same degree: Indeed, some physically fit senior citizens easily outperform middle-aged individuals who lead sedentary lifestyles. Nevertheless, when designing a store, take such issues and changes into consideration.

A helpful tool is the Age Explorer. It consists of a suit and a helmet that provides the wearer with a first-hand impression of the physical limitations associated with aging. A young person wearing this suit is in for a treat of an experience, such as instant arthritis (simulated by tiny needles in the gloves), a restricted field of vision, hearing problems, decreased muscle strength, and stiffer limbs and joints. It is indeed a special time machine that can be used to test how an older person might feel in your store. Such age exploration in a retail store is illustrated in Figure 7.3.

Even if you don't have an Age Explorer on hand, you can still take measures to make shopping easier and more pleasant for your mature consumers:

- Use high-contrast colors (ideally reds and yellows).
- Ensure that lights in the store are bright, but ideally glare free; indirect illumination should be used.

Figure 7.3. Using the Age Explorer is a good way to make your store more accessible to mature shoppers.

- Avoid shiny and reflective surfaces.
- Use only nonslip flooring.
- Use large letters on signage to ensure legibility for everyone.
- Illuminate and clearly label any hazards in the store.
- Avoid steep stairs.
- In addition to stairs, plan for elevators and (slow-moving) escalators.
- Provide rest areas throughout the store.
- Adjust the volume of background music to a (low) volume suitable for more mature shoppers.

Whatever measures you take, do not single out or stereotype mature shoppers. Interestingly, most consumers in the age group that is 60 and older feel considerably younger than they actually are. In a study conducted among healthy senior citizens (the ones that would shop at your store), we found that their cognitive age (how old they feel) was a surprising 12 years younger than their biological age.[10] When communicating with mature shoppers (e.g., with in-store graphics), keep this fact in mind. Mature shoppers can be a very rewarding target group for many retailers—but only if their special needs and interests are taken into consideration and respected fully.

Recipe 4: Keep Shoppers in Your Store Longer

The longer a shopper stays in a store, the higher the likelihood that she will make (additional) purchases. So the crucial question then becomes, what measures can be taken to make customers stay around longer? In truth, store environment considerably influences whether a customer browses longer than she initially intended. A retailer can take several actions to keep shoppers longer in the store:

- Reduce walking speed. Shoppers will walk more slowly if they listen to soft music and walk on a soft floor.
- Adjust music to your target group. Shoppers will leave a store early if they listen to music they are not familiar with. For example, use Top 40 music in a fashion store and classical music in an upscale wine store.

- Avoid crowding. Shoppers will leave a store if they are confronted with crowded situations. Therefore, allocate enough space to areas that have a risk of crowding.
- Entertain those who accompany shoppers. Provide comfortable seats and magazines and other forms of entertainment near fitting rooms in order to avoid bored partners or friends. Additionally, provide an area where children can play. A supervised kid's corner will allow parents to do their shopping in a more relaxed spirit.
- Communicate to all shoppers that they will miss out on something great if they do not visit all areas of the store. This communication can be achieved either by a loop or by appropriate in-store graphics. Emotional pictures act as eye-catchers and lure shoppers to less frequented areas of a store.
- Make the customer feel at ease. Provide relaxing zones, such as in-store cafés, as well as restrooms, water coolers, and other conveniences.
- Use deactivating stimuli when shoppers are stressed. For example, plants, water, and the color green put shoppers in a calm spirit.
- Provide areas where shoppers can try their products. For example, in a music store, customers often like to listen to selected songs before they purchase them.

Whatever you do, keeping shoppers in your store longer is not enough. Only when this time translates into additional contact with the merchandise will you see an actual increase in sales.

Recipe 5: Trigger Impulse Purchases

Who doesn't know about the secret persuaders at the supermarket checkout area that silently, by their very presence, convince shoppers to reward themselves for a successful shopping trip? Candy, snacks, or magazines are effective impulse items and may be the last chance to increase sales before the shopper leaves the store. In fact, in a recent study 60% of adult women stated they bought items just on a whim. Interestingly, these items were not exactly inexpensive; the average sum of the last impulse purchase was $108, a nontrivial amount.[11] Obviously, this sum cannot only be buying items located in the checkout area. Instead, a store gains from influencing impulse purchases in the entire store. Here are a few suggestions on how to do just that:

- *Point-of-purchase displays.* Both content displays that inform shoppers of certain benefits of a product (e.g., a body lotion can praise its smooth effect) and product supply displays that attract shopper attention can be used. Additionally, a food store can use promotion booths that offer samples to whet a shopper's appetite. Product sampling is also an option for many other types of stores.

- *Use novel, unusual, and high-contrast stimuli.* Shoppers will not search for impulse purchases like they do for products they intend to buy. Therefore, extra effort is needed to draw a shopper's attention to impulse items. This can be done by highlighting impulse purchase zones with brighter colors,[12] additional lighting, or unusual decorations. Keep in mind, however, that the products you designate as impulse items must in fact fit this purpose. Grabbing the shopper's attention won't help if the highlighted item isn't a product most shoppers are willing to purchase spontaneously. We learned this lesson when we developed an innovative product display for a client. Whenever shoppers passed by this point-of-purchase display, from a hidden speaker a recorded voice whispered, "Pssst!" The display sure got a lot of attention. Unfortunately, its effect on sales was negligible. What was the problem? The highlighted product—socks. In the store where we tried out the whispering display, these were clearly not bought on impulse. Fortunately, the display has since been used for other products, and impulse purchases of the promoted products have indeed increased.

- *Verbal prompting.* Some time ago we conducted a study to find out how impulse purchases can be increased in fast-food stores. We instructed the staff to ask customers if they wanted a side dish added to their main course (e.g.,

"Would you like potato salad with that order?"). This type of suggestion yielded a considerable increase in sales for side dishes.[13] Verbal prompting can be used in a retail setting as well. Every time a shopper interacts with sales staff, special offers or the latest innovations can be mentioned. Additionally, prompting can also be done through visual cues. For example, display signs indicating which other items can be used in combination with another product (e.g., show a picture near a couch to indicate which pillows match the couch design).

- *Present products with companion items.* Bundled presentations show shoppers how products can be used in real life. A customer who planned to buy wine glasses might also buy table decorations or other tableware if all these products are so appealingly arranged that the shopper cannot resist.

However, there is also a dark side to impulse purchases. In a study, 35% of women who made an impulse purchase in a drugstore stated that they regretted what they impulsively bought over the last 12 months.[14] Therefore, especially for impulse items, appropriate actions to reduce after-purchase regret should be taken. This could be done by confirming the good purchase decision either through the sales staff or by adding printed statements inside the packaging like "Congratulations on your purchase—you just bought the lipstick of the year."

Recipe 6: Create A-to-Z Shopping Conveniences That Will Work for Your Store

In this section of our store cookbook, you won't find a full recipe. Instead, you'll find a starter list of ingredients to use to make shopping more convenient for each of your customers (Table 7.1). See which ones you can add to your store or mall at a justifiable cost. Then think of others and complete your own A-to-Z personal shopping conveniences list that is precisely focused to your store and your customers.

Table 7.1. Shopping Conveniences Your Customers Might Appreciate

Arcade games	Parking lot
Bag lockers	Pet corner
Call buttons for sales clerks (see Figure 7.4)	Price scanner
Courtesy phones	Ramps for easy access
Diaper changing station	Restaurant
Disinfectant wipes for shopping cart	Restrooms
Elevator	Scooters
Escalator	Seats for breaks
Electronic bridal registry	Self-checkout
Fitting rooms	Shopping baskets
Gloves for handling merchandise	Store-specific app for smartphone
Information desk	Umbrella bags
In-store café	Vending machines
Interactive information kiosk	Waiting area for spouses
Kid's corner	Waiting ticket dispenser
Magnifying glass affixed to shelves	Water cooler
Managed checkout line	Wi-Fi
Meeting points	You-are-here map

Figure 7.4. A call button to summon sales clerks is considered a convenience by most shoppers.

Recipe 7: Place Your Shoppers in a Constant State of Flow

What do all the following people have in common?

- A rock climber mastering a challenging route (see Figure 7.5)
- An expert chess player immerged in a difficult game
- A music enthusiast mastering a complex piece on the piano
- A gamer playing a computer game for hours on end
- A marketing expert writing a book on store design into the wee hours of the morning

They are all experiencing the mental state of flow. According to psychologist Mihaly Csikszentmihalyi, people are in a mental flow when they are totally involved in an enjoyable activity for its own sake. When we are in a state of flow, we fully concentrate on the task at hand. People in a state of flow also experience a feeling of happiness. Flow, however, is more than just a passive pleasure, such as watching a great movie or enjoying a good glass of wine. To experience flow, which is a much stronger form of happiness, a person must be inherently active and involved. Flow derives

Figure 7.5. Sportler, a sports equipment store in Treviso, Italy, provides customers with a man-made rock wall—a great way to place them in a state of flow.

from mastering a task for which someone has the appropriate skill set. The right balance of challenge and skills is important, as is receiving clear and immediate feedback. When in a state of flow, people are exhilarated, feel a sense of accomplishment, and frequently lose track of time.[15]

It would be unrealistic to expect all shoppers to experience flow every time they are in a store no matter how that store is designed. We can, however, take certain measures that will increase the likelihood of that flow occurring in a store. After all, shopping can on occasion be truly enjoyable and even challenging: Finding that perfect gift for a loved one or canvassing a flea market for that special antique that everyone else neglects to recognize and buy are just two activities that can put consumers in a state of flow.

Let's see how flow-inducing elements can be integrated in a store by using the example of a furniture store:[16]

1. After entering the store, facilities for the safekeeping of bags (lockers) as well as children (a children's corner where children can play under supervision) can free shoppers from undue distractions and help them concentrate on making the most optimal purchases.

2. By presenting products as part of bundled presentations (in fully equipped rooms instead of separately by category) the shopper is encouraged to think about products that complement one another.

3. On computer terminals, customers can use their personal creativity to plan the interior design of their rooms, using simple, intuitive software. Available sales staff can help whenever necessary.

4. Signs can encourage shoppers to experiment and combine furniture and decorations according to their individual tastes or try something new and unusual.

5. In the bargain corner right before checkout, customers can gain an additional sense of accomplishment by finding special deals at significantly reduced prices.

6. Finally, at the end of a shopping trip, depending on their skill level and desired degree of involvement, shoppers can rent vehicles to take the furniture home themselves or arrange to have it delivered to meet their best schedule; they can also decide to assemble the furniture themselves to achieve personal satisfaction or have it assembled by the store staff as an extra help.

Perhaps some of these steps can also be used in your store to place your customers in a state of flow.

Takeaway Points

Here are the most important takeaway points from this chapter:

- Customers hate waiting. Make them happy (and your store more profitable) by influencing their perception of waiting time.
- Use store design and visual merchandising techniques to influence price perceptions.
- Design your store to fit the specific needs of senior citizens— this will make it more accessible and convenient for all shoppers.
- Use store design to keep shoppers in your store longer. This can translate into additional sales.
- Many purchase decisions are made in the store. Design your store to encourage unplanned purchases.
- Consider every possible way to make shopping more convenient for your customers.
- Place your shoppers in a state of flow.

Notes

Introduction

1. Morin (1983).

Chapter 1

1. Packard (1958), p. 92.
2. Ebster, Koppler, Rath, and Reiterer (2010).
3. Underhill (1999).
4. Underhill (1999).
5. Underhill (1999).
6. Groeppel-Klein and Bartmann (2009).
7. Underhill (1999), p. 17.
8. Ebster, Wagner, and Valis (2006).
9. Berman and Evans (2007).
10. Bajaj, Srivastava, and Tuli (2005).
11. Berman and Evans (2007).
12. Kreft (1993).
13. Lewison (1991).
14. Barr and Broudy (1986).
15. Henderson and Hollingworth (1999).
16. Magee (2010).
17. Packaging Research (1983).
18. Sanders (1963).
19. Ebster, Wagner, and Neumueller (2009).
20. Chandon, Hutchinson, Bradlow, and Young (2009).
21. Chandon, Hutchinson, Bradlow, and Young (2009).
22. Sorensen (2009).
23. Sorensen (2009).
24. Deherder and Blatt (2010).

Chapter 2

1. Wal-Mart (2010).
2. Tolman (1984).

3. Lynch (1960).
4. Sommer and Aitkens (1982).
5. Golledge (2004).
6. Grossbart and Rammohan (1981).
7. Berger (2005).
8. Miller (1956).
9. Carroll (2010).
10. Bix (2002).
11. Illiteracy (2007).
12. Blackwood (2002).
13. Paivio (1991).
14. Childers and Houston (1984); Groeppel-Klein and Germelmann (2003).
15. Gifford (1997).
16. Solomon, Bamossy, Askegaard, and Hogg (2006).

Chapter 3

1. Churchill (1943).
2. Moore, Doherty, and Doyle (2010).
3. Storefronts (1996).
4. Citrin, Stem, Spangenberg, and Clark (2003).
5. Van der Waerden, Borgers, and Timmermans (1998).
6. Citrin, Stem, Spangenberg, and Clark (2003).
7. Falk (2003).
8. Kardes, Cline, and Cronley (2011).
9. Dabholkar, Bobbitt, and Lee (2003).
10. Lovelock and Wirtz (2011); Mills (n.d.).
11. Dabholkar, Bobbitt, and Lee (2003).
12. Dolliver (2009).
13. Hui and Bateson (1991).
14. Taylor (2004).
15. Taylor (2004).
16. Haarlander (2001).
17. Falk (2003).
18. Haarlander (2001); Meyer, Harris, Kohns, Stone, and Ashmun (1988).
19. Falk (2003).
20. Taylor (2004).
21. Haarlander (2001); Meyer, Harris, Kohns, Stone, and Ashmun (1988).
22. O'Connell (2008).
23. Buttle (1984).
24. Sen, Block, and Chandran (2002).
25. Falk (2003).

26. O'Shea (2003).
27. Falk (2003).
28. Sen, Block, and Chandran (2002).
29. Bolen (1988).
30. Falk (2003).
31. Buttle (1984).
32. Buber, Ruso, and Gadner (2006).
33. Falk (2003).
34. Falk (2003), p. 74.
35. Kotler and Armstrong (2010).
36. Bolen (1988).
37. Karana, Hekkert, and Kandachar (2009).
38. Ebster, Wagner, and Geider (2008).
39. Turley and Milliman (2000).
40. Citrin, Stem, Spangenberg, and Clark (2003).
41. Wedel and Pieters (2008).
42. Araba (2004); Karana (2010); Karana, Hekkert, and Kandachar (2009); Wedel and Pieters (2008).
43. Wedel and Pieters (2008).
44. Buttle (1984).
45. Vence (2007).
46. Lash (1998).
47. Lash (1998).
48. McKinnon, Kelly, and Robison (1981).
49. Cornelius, Natter, and Faure (2010).
50. Lewison (1991).
51. Cooper (2010).
52. Sands (1984).
53. Buttle (1984).
54. Meyer, Harris, Kohns, Stone, and Ashmun (1988).
55. Buttle (1984).
56. Levy and Weitz (2009).
57. Meyer, Harris, Kohns, Stone, and Ashmun (1988).
58. Chandon, Hutchinson, Bradlow, and Young (2009).
59. Mills (n.d.).
60. Mills (n.d.).
61. Wedel and Pieters (2008).
62. Araba (2004).
63. Catchpole (1995).
64. Hornik (1992).
65. Tips (1995).
66. Wedel and Pieters (2008).
67. Grewal, Baker, Levy, and Voss (2003).

68. Barbaro (2007).
69. Levy and Weitz (2009).
70. Dabholkar, Bobbitt, and Lee (2003).

Chapter 4

1. Allenby and Lenk (1995).
2. Depaoli (1992).
3. Kardes, Cline, and Cronley (2011).
4. Iyengar (2010).
5. Iyengar and Lepper (2000).
6. Kowitt (2010).
7. Bhalla and Anuraag (2010).
8. Bastow-Shoop, Zetocha, and Passewitz (1991).
9. Bastow-Shoop, Zetocha, and Passewitz (1991).
10. Bhalla and Anuraag (2010).
11. Colborne (1996).
12. Bellenger, Robertson, and Hirschman (1978).
13. Abrahams (1997).
14. Groeppel (1991).
15. Groeppel (1991).
16. Ebster and Jandrisits (2003).
17. Bhalla and Anuraag (2010).
18. Wilkie (1994).
19. Wilkie (1994).
20. Bost (1987).
21. Kroeber-Riel (1993).
22. Booker (2004).
23. Traindl (2007).
24. Ebster and Reisinger (2005).
25. Berlyne (1971).
26. Veryzer and Hutchinson (1998).
27. Bhalla and Anuraag (2010).
28. Bell and Ternus (2002).
29. Bell and Ternus (2002).
30. Bell and Ternus (2002).
31. Curhan (1974).
32. Kahn and Wansink (2004).
33. Wertheimer (1922).
34. Bell and Ternus (2002).
35. Crowley (1991).
36. Wertheimer (1922).
37. Depaoli (1992).

Chapter 5

1. Baker, Grewal, and Parasuraman (1994).
2. Turley and Milliman (2000).
3. Mehrabian and Russell (1974).
4. Russell and Mehrabian (1976).
5. Donovan and Rossiter (1982).
6. Baker, Grewal, and Levy (1992).
7. Berlyne (1971).
8. Bost (1987).
9. Donovan, Rossiter, Marcoolyn, and Nesdale (1994).
10. Spies, Hesse, and Loesch (1997).
11. Donovan and Rossiter (1982); Spies, Hesse, and Loesch (1997).
12. Donovan, Rossiter, Marcoolyn, and Nesdale (1994).
13. Donovan and Rossiter (1982).
14. Donovan and Rossiter (1982); Spies, Hesse, and Loesch (1997).
15. Chebat, Chebat, and Vaillant (2001).
16. Milliman (1986).
17. Yalch and Spangenberg (1990).
18. Milliman (1982).
19. Milliman (1982).
20. Sweeney and Wyber (2002).
21. Areni and Kim (1993).
22. Yalch and Spangenberg (1990).
23. Yalch and Spangenberg (1988).
24. Chebat, Chebat, and Vaillant (2001); Stratton and Zalanowski (1984).
25. MacInnis and Park (1991).
26. Glamser (1990).
27. Kubota (2009).
28. Brookes (2005).
29. Wilkie (1995).
30. Haugtvedt, Herr, and Kardes (2008).
31. Burling (2006).
32. Ebster and Jandrisits (2003).
33. Burling (2006).
34. Spangenberg, Crowley, and Henderson (1996).
35. Hirsch (1995).
36. Ebster and Jandrisits (2003).
37. Chebat and Michon (2003).
38. Pepper (1993).
39. Chebat and Michon (2003).
40. Ebster and Kirk-Smith (2005).
41. Russell and Mehrabian (1976).

42. Biner, Butler, Fischer, and Westergren (1989).
43. Areni and Kim (1994).
44. Summers (2001).
45. Barr and Broudy (1986).
46. Barr and Broudy (1986).
47. Exhibit (1996).
48. Bellizzi, Crowley, and Hasty (1983).
49. Crowley (1993).
50. Crowley (1993).
51. Babin, Hardesty, and Suter (2003).
52. Bellizzi, Crowley, and Hasty (1983).
53. Crowley (1993).
54. Crowley (1993).
55. Machleit, Eroglu, and Mantel (2000).
56. Hui and Bateson (1991).
57. Harrell, Hutt, and Anderson (1980).
58. Mitchell, Kahn, and Knasko (1995).
59. Ebster and Jandrisits (2003).
60. Mattila and Wirtz (2001).
61. Baker, Drewel, and Levy (1992).
62. Mattila and Wirtz (2001).
63. Machleit, Eroglu, and Mantel (2000).

Chapter 6

1. Grewal, Levy, and Kumar (2009).
2. Smilansky (2009).
3. Bellizzi and Hite (1992).
4. Arnold and Reynolds (2003); Batra and Ahtola (1991).
5. Arnold and Reynolds (2003); Babin, Darden, and Griffin (1994).
6. Forsythe and Bailey (1996).
7. Arnold and Reynolds (2003).
8. Pine and Gilmore (1999).
9. Buss (2002), p. 82.
10. Falk (2003).
11. Leonard (2008).
12. O'Neill (2009).
13. Oldenburg (1999), pp. 14–17.
14. Ebster (2009).
15. Granbois (1968).
16. Borges, Chebat, and Babin (2010).
17. Penn and Zalesne (2007).

18. Dodes (2005).
19. Clarke (2005).
20. Dunn, Aknin, and Norton (2008).
21. Gone tomorrow (2009).
22. Weinberg (1992).
23. Shakespeare (2009), p. 38
24. Goffman (1959).
25. Lovelock and Morgan (1996), p. 133.
26. Grove and Fisk (1983).
27. McGoun, Dunkak, Bettner, and Allen (2003).
28. Mitrasinovic (1998).
29. Henderson (1999).
30. Bryman (2004).
31. Nation (1998).
32. Spector (1999).
33. Bryman (2004).
34. Dunlop (1996); Mongello (2006).
35. Schmitt and Simonson (1997).
36. Alcorn (2010).
37. Trilling (1972).
38. Eco (1986).
39. Ebster and Guist (2005).

Chapter 7

1. Casey (2004).
2. Doyle (2003).
3. Barnes (2010).
4. Maister (1984).
5. Lovelock and Wirtz (2011).
6. Ebster (2006).
7. Smith and Burns (1996).
8. Vincent and Velkoff (2010).
9. Vincent and Velkoff (2010).
10. Ebster, Wagner, and Sperl (2011).
11. Dolliver (2009).
12. Rook and Hoch (1985).
13. Ebster, Wagner, and Valis (2006).
14. Dolliver (2009).
15. Csikszentmihalyi (1990).
16. Drott (2006).

References

Abrahams, B. (1997). It's all in the mind. *Marketing, 27*, 31–33.

Alcorn, S. (2010). *Theme park design.* Orlando, FL: Theme Perks Inc.

Allenby, G. M., & Lenk, P. J. (1995). Reassessing brand loyalty, price sensitivity, and merchandising effects on consumer brand choice. *Journal of Business & Economic Statistics, 13*(3), 281–289.

Angermann, E. (Ed.). (1989). *Das Handbuch der Marktforschung.* Wien, Austria: Signum.

Araba, K. C. (2004, March 2). Material's central role in product personality. *Industry Market Trends.* Retrieved from http://news.thomasnet.com/IMT/archives/2004/03/materials_centr.html

Areni, C. S., & Kim, D. (1993). The influence of background music on shopping behavior: Classical versus top-forty music in a wine store. *Advances in Consumer Research, 20*, 336–340.

Areni, C. S., & Kim, D. (1994). The influence of in-store lighting on consumers' examination of merchandise in a wine store. *International Journal of Marketing, 11*(2), 117–127.

Arnold, M. J., & Reynolds, K. E. (2003). Hedonic shopping motivations. *Journal of Retailing, 79*(2), 77–95.

Babin, B. J., Darden, W. R., & Griffin, M. (1994). Work and/or fun: Measuring hedonic and utilitarian shopping value. *The Journal of Consumer Research, 20*(4), 644–656.

Babin, B. J., Hardesty, D. M., & Suter, T. A. (2003). Color and shopping intentions: The intervening effect of price fairness and perceived affect. *Journal of Business Research, 56*(7), 541–551.

Bajaj, C., Srivastava, N. V., & Tuli, R. (2005). *Retail management.* New Delhi, India: Oxford University Press.

Baker, J., Grewal, D., & Levy, M. (1992). An experimental approach to making retail store decisions. *Journal of Retailing, 68*(4), 445–460.

Baker, J., Grewal, D., & Parasuraman, A. (1994). The influence of store environment on quality inferences and store image. *Journal of the Academy of Marketing Science, 22*(4), 328–339.

Barbaro, M. (2007, June 23). A long line for a shorter wait at the supermarket. *The New York Times,* p. 1.

Barnes, B. (2010, December 28). Disney technology tackles a theme-park headache: Lines. *The New York Times,* p. 1.

Barr, V., & Broudy, C. E. (1986). *Designing to sell: A complete guide to retail store planning and design*. New York, NY: McGraw-Hill.

Bastow-Shoop, H., Zetocha, D., & Passewitz, G. (1991). *Visual merchandising: A guide for small retailers*. Ames, IA: North Central Regional Center for Rural Development.

Batra, R., & Ahtola, O. T. (1991). Measuring the hedonic and utilitarian sources of consumer attitudes. *Marketing Letters, 2*(2), 159–170.

Bell, J. A., & Ternus, K. (2002). *Silent selling: Best practices and effective strategies in visual merchandising* (2nd ed.). New York, NY: Fairchild Publications.

Bellenger, D. N., Robertson, D. H., & Hirschman, E. C. (1978). Impulse buying varies by product. *Journal of Advertising Research, 18*(6), 15–18.

Bellizzi, J. A., Crowley, A. E., & Hasty, R. W. (1983). The effects of color in store design. *Journal of Retailing, 59*(1), 21–45.

Bellizzi, J. A., & Hite, R. E. (1992). Environmental color, consumer feelings and purchase likelihood. *Psychology & Marketing, 9*(5), 347–363.

Berger, C. (2005). *Wayfinding: Designing and implementing graphic navigational systems*. Mies, Switzerland: RotoVision.

Berlyne, D. E. (1971). *Aesthetics and psychobiology*. New York, NY: Appleton-Century-Croft.

Berman, B., & Evans, J. R. (2007). *Retail management: A strategic approach* (10th ed.). Upper Saddle River, NJ: Pearson/Prentice Hall.

Bhalla, S., & Anuraag, S. (2010). *Visual merchandising*. New Delhi, India: Tata McGraw-Hill.

Biner, P. M., Butler, D. L., Fischer, A. R., & Westergren, A. J. (1989). An arousal optimization model of lighting level preferences: An interaction of social situation and task demands. *Environment and Behavior, 21*(1), 3–16.

Bix, L. (2002, Spring). The elements of text and message design and their impact on message legibility: A literature review. *Journal of Design Communication*. Retrieved from http://scholar.lib.vt.edu/ejournals/JDC/Spring-2002/bix.html

Blackwood, A. (2002). Good signs. *Buildings, 96*(10), 2.

Bolen, W. H. (1988). *Contemporary retailing* (3rd ed.). Englewood Cliffs, NJ: Prentice Hall.

Booker, C. (2004). *The seven basic plots: Why we tell stories*. London, UK: Continuum.

Borges, A., Chebat, J.-C., & Babin, B. J. (2010). Does a companion always enhance the shopping experience? *Journal of Retailing and Consumer Services, 17*(4), 294–299.

Bost, E. (1987). *Ladenatmosphäre und Konsumentenverhalten. Konsum und Verhalten*. Heidelberg, Germany: Physica-Verlag.

Brookes, B. (2005, June 17). Double standards: "Don't call in-store radio background noise." *Campaign*, 14.

Bryman, A. (2004). *The Disneyization of society*. Thousand Oaks, CA: Sage.

Buber, R., Ruso, B., & Gadner, J. (2006). Evolutionäres Design von Verkaufsräumen: Wasser, Pflanzen, Tier und Sichtschutz als verhaltenssteuernde Gestaltungselemente. In P. Schnedlitz, R. Buber, T. Reutterer, A. Schuh, & C. Teller (Eds.), *Innovationen in Marketing und Handel* (pp. 361–378). Wien, Austria: Linde Verlag.

Burling, S. (2006, October 30). Shopper study: Do smells sell? *The Philadelphia Inquirer*, p. D01.

Buss, D. (2002, January 28). Dealers make showrooms an "experience." *Automotive News*, 82.

Buttle, F. (1984). Retail space allocation. *International Journal of Physical Distribution & Materials Management, 14*(4), 3–23.

Carroll, M. J. (2010). *Design resources: DR-11 text legibility and readability of large format signs in buildings and sites*. Buffalo, NY: Center for Inclusive Design and Environmental Access, University of Buffalo.

Casey, B. (2004). Convenience intensifies cross-channel competition. *Drug Store News, 26*(2), 16.

Catchpole, K. (1995, February). The great mirror mystery. *Allure*. Retrieved from http://www.truemirror.com/press/html%5Ctmc_allure.0295.asp

Chandon, P., Hutchinson, J. W., Bradlow, E. T., & Young, S. H. (2009). Does in-store marketing work? Effects of the number and position of shelf facings on brand attention and evaluation at the point of purchase. *Journal of Marketing, 73*(6), 1–17.

Chebat, J.-C., Chebat, C. G., & Vaillant, D. (2001). Environmental background music and in-store selling. *Journal of Business Research, 54*(2), 115–123.

Chebat, J.-C., & Michon, R. (2003). Impact of ambient odors on mall shoppers' emotions, cognition, and spending: A test of competitive causal theories. *Journal of Business Research, 56*(7), 529–539.

Childers, T. L., & Houston, M. J. (1984). Conditions for a picture-superiority effect on consumer memory. *The Journal of Consumer Research, 11*(2), 643–654.

Churchill, W. S. (1943, October 28). Speech to the House of Commons.

Citrin, A. V., Stem, D. E., Spangenberg, E. R., & Clark, M. J. (2003). Consumer need for tactile input: An internet retailing challenge: Strategy in e-marketing. *Journal of Business Research, 56*(11), 915–922.

Clarke, J. (2005). The four S's of experience gift giving behaviour. *Hospitality Management, 26*(1), 98–116.

Colborne, R. (1996). *Visual merchandising: The business of merchandise presentation*. Albany, NY: Delmar Publishers.

Cooper, L. (2010, October 7). Point of purchase: Bright ideas on final steps of purchase path. *Marketing Week*. Retrieved from http://www.marketingweek.co.uk/analysis/features/bright-ideas-on-final-steps-of-purchase-path/3018978.article

Cornelius, B., Natter, M., & Faure, C. (2010). How storefront displays influence retail store image. *Journal of Retailing and Consumer Services, 17*(2), 143–151.

Crowley, A. E. (1991). The golden section. *Psychology & Marketing, 8*(2), 101–116.

Crowley, A. E. (1993). The two-dimensional impact of color on shopping. *Marketing Letters, 4*(1), 59–69.

Csikszentmihalyi, M. (1990). *Flow: The psychology of optimal experience.* New York, NY: Harper & Row.

Curhan, R. C. (1974). The effects of merchandising and temporary promotional activities on the sales of fresh fruits and vegetables in supermarkets. *Journal of Marketing Research, 11*(3), 286.

Dabholkar, P. A., Bobbitt, M. L., & Lee, E.-J. (2003). Understanding consumer motivation and behavior related to self-scanning in retailing. *International Journal of Service Industry Management, 14*(1), 59–95.

Deherder, R., & Blatt, R. (2010). *Shopper intimacy: A practical guide to leveraging marketing intelligence to drive retail success.* Upper Saddle River, NJ: FT Press.

Depaoli, M. A. (1992). *Die Sprache der Ware: Zukunftsorientierte Produktpräsentation, angewandtes Merchandising.* Wien, Austria: Uberreuter.

Dodes, R. (2005, February 13). O.K., it's over. So now let's party. *The New York Times*, p. 1.

Dolliver, M. (2009, November 20). Impulse buying is alive and well. *Progressive Grocer.* Retrieved from http://www.progressivegrocer.com/top-story-impulse_buying_is_alive_and_well-26290.html

Donovan, R. J., & Rossiter, J. R. (1982). Store atmosphere: An environmental psychology approach. *Journal of Retailing, 58*(1), 34.

Donovan, R. J., Rossiter, J. R., Marcoolyn, G., & Nesdale, A. (1994). Store atmosphere and purchasing behavior. *Journal of Retailing, 70*(3), 283–294.

Doyle, M. (2003). Fighting back with convenience. *Progressive Grocer, 82*(6), 20–24.

Drott, C. (2006). *Flow im Erlebniskauf.* Market Mentor archive #294.

Dunlop, B. (1996). *Building a dream: The art of Disney architecture.* New York, NY: Abrams.

Dunn, E. W., Aknin, L. B., & Norton, M. I. (2008). Spending money on others promotes happiness. *Science, 319*(5870), 1687–1688.

Ebster, C. (2006). UCI Kinowelt: Optimierung des Wartebereichs. In U. Wagner, H. Reisinger, C. Schwand, & D. Hoppe (Eds.), *Fallstudien aus der österreichischen Marketingpraxis* (pp. 51–59). Wien, Austria: WUV.

Ebster, C. (2009). Starbucks: A legendary experience at a steep price. In U. Wagner, H. Reisinger, & C. Schwand (Eds.), *Fallstudien aus der österreichischen Marketingpraxis* (5th ed., pp. 197–205). Wien, Austria: WUV.

Ebster, C., & Guist, I. (2005). The role of authenticity in ethnic theme restaurants. *Journal of Foodservice Business Research, 7*(2), 41–52.

Ebster, C., & Jandrisits, M. (2003). Die Wirkung kongruenten Duftes auf die Stimmung des Konsumenten am Point of Sale. *Marketing ZFP, 25*(2), 99–106.

Ebster, C., & Kirk-Smith, M. (2005). The effect of the human pheromone androstenol on product evaluation. *Psychology & Marketing, 22*(9), 739–749.

Ebster, C., Koppler, B., Rath, D., & Reiterer, B. (2010). Shadowing study. Market Mentor archive #486.

Ebster, C., & Reisinger, H. (2005). How attractive should a salesperson be? Results of an experimental study. *Finanza Marketing e Produzione, 23*(3), 124–130.

Ebster, C., Wagner, U., & Neumueller, D. (2009). Children's influences on in-store purchases. *Journal of Retailing and Consumer Services, 16*(2), 145–154.

Ebster, C., Wagner, U., & Valis, S. (2006). The effectiveness of verbal prompts on sales. *Journal of Retailing and Consumer Services, 13*(3), 169–176.

Ebster, C., Wagner, U., & Geider, B. (2008). *The effect of floor texture on consumer behaviour at the point of sale.* Proceedings of the 2008 Society for Marketing Advances Conference, St. Petersburg, FL.

Ebster, C., Wagner, U., & Sperl, S. (2011). Cognitive age. Working paper. Department of Marketing, University of Vienna.

Eco, U. (1986). *Travels in hyperreality.* New York, NY: Harcourt Brace Jovanovich.

Exhibit. (1996, July 2). Exhibit to highlight in-store lighting. *Business World,* 14.

Falk, E. A. (2003). *1001 ideas to create retail excitement* (rev. ed.). New York, NY: Prentice Hall.

Forsythe, S. M., & Bailey, A. W. (1996). Shopping enjoyment, perceived time poverty, and time spent shopping. *Clothing and Textiles Research Journal, 14*(3), 185–191.

Gifford, R. (1997). *Environmental psychology: Principles and practice* (2nd ed.). Boston, MA: Allyn and Bacon.

Glamser, D. (1990), August 24). Mozart plays the empty lot. *USA Today,* p. 3a.

Goffman, E. (1959). *The presentation of self in everyday life.* New York, NY: Anchor Books.

Golledge, R. G. (2004). Human wayfinding and cognitive maps. In A. Bailly & L. Gibson (Eds.), *Applied geography: A world perspective* (pp. 233–252). Dordrecht, Netherlands: Kluwer Academic.

Gone tomorrow. (2009, July 23). Gone tomorrow: The spread of pop-up retailing. *The Economist* (U.S. ed.). Retrieved from http://www.economist.com/node/14101585

Gottdiener, M. (1997). *The theming of America: Dreams, visions, and commercial spaces.* Boulder, CO: Westview Press.

Granbois, D. H. (1968). Improving the study of customer in-store behavior. *The Journal of Marketing, 32*(4), 28–33.

Grewal, D., Baker, J., Levy, M., & Voss, G. B. (2003). The effects of wait expectations and store atmosphere evaluations on patronage intentions in service-intensive retail stores. *Journal of Retailing, 79*(4), 259–268.

Grewal, D., Levy, M., & Kumar, V. (2009). Customer experience management in retailing: An organizing framework: Enhancing the retail customer experience. *Journal of Retailing, 85*(1), 1–14.

Groeppel, A. (1991). *Erlebnisstrategien im Einzelhandel: Analyse der Zielgruppen, der Ladengestaltung und der Warenpräsentation zur Vermittlung von Einkaufserlebnissen. Konsum und Verhalten*. Heidelberg, Germany: Physica-Verlag.

Groeppel-Klein, A., & Bartmann, B. (2009). Turning bias and walking patterns: Consumers' orientation in a discount store. *Marketing: Journal of Research and Management, 29*(1), 41–56.

Groeppel-Klein, A., & Germelmann, C. C. (2003). "Minding the mall": Do we remember what we see? *Advances in Consumer Research, 30*, 56–67.

Grossbart, S. L., & Rammohan, B. (1981). Cognitive maps and shopping convenience. *Advances in Consumer Research, 8*, 128–133.

Grove, S. J., & Fisk, R. P. (1983). The dramaturgy of services exchange: An analytical framework for services marketing. In L. L. Berry, G. L. Shostack, & G. D. Upah (Eds.), *Emerging perspectives on services marketing* (45–49). Chicago, IL: American Marketing Association.

Haarlander, L. (2001, May 7). Does your sign make a good impression? Here are a few tips on making signage work. *Buffalo News*, p. D1.

Harrell, G. D., Hutt, M. D., & Anderson, J. D. (1980). Path analysis of buyer behavior under conditions of crowding. *Journal of Marketing Research, 17*(1), 45–51.

Haugtvedt, C. P., Herr, P. M., & Kardes, F. R. (Eds.). (2008). *Handbook of consumer psychology*. New York, NY: Psychology Press.

Henderson, J. (1999). *Casino design: Resorts, hotels, and themed entertainment spaces*. Gloucester, MA: Quarry Books.

Henderson, J. M., & Hollingworth, A. (1999). High-level scene perception. *Annual Review of Psychology, 50*(1), 243–271.

Hirsch, A. (1995). Effect of ambient odors on slot machine usage in a Las Vegas casino. *Psychology & Marketing, 12*(7), 585–594.

Hornik, J. (1992). Tactile stimulation and consumer response. *The Journal of Consumer Research, 19*(3), 449–458.

Hui, M. K., & Bateson, J. E. (1991). Perceived control and the effects of crowding and consumer choice on the service experience. *Journal of Consumer Research, 18*(2), 174–184.

Hunter, B. T. (1995). The sale appeal of scents (using synthetic food scents to increase sales). *Consumers' Research Magazine, 78*(10), 8–9.

Illiteracy. (2007). Illiteracy: The downfall of American society. Retrieved from http://education-portal.com/articles/Illiteracy:_The_Downfall_of_American_Society.html

Iyengar, S. S. (2010). *The art of choosing* (1st ed.). New York, NY: Twelve.

Iyengar, S. S., & Lepper, M. R. (2000). When choice is demotivating: Can one desire too much of a good thing? *Journal of Personality and Social Psychology, 79*(6), 995–1006.

Kahn, B. E., & Wansink, B. (2004). The influence of assortment structure on perceived variety and consumption quantities. *Journal of Consumer Research, 30*(4), 519–533.

Kanner, B. (1989, April 3). Color schemes. *New York Magazine,* 22–23.

Karana, E. (2010). How do materials obtain their meanings? *Middle East Technical University Journal of the Faculty of Architecture, 2*(27), 271–285.

Karana, E., Hekkert, P., & Kandachar, P. (2009). Meanings of materials through sensorial properties and manufacturing processes. *Materials and Design, 30*(7), 2779–2784.

Kardes, F. R., Cline, T. W., & Cronley, M. L. (2011). *Consumer behavior: Science and practice.* Mason, OH: South-Western Cengage Learning.

Kotler, P., & Armstrong, G. (2010). *Principles of marketing* (13th ed.). Upper Saddle River, NJ: Pearson.

Kowitt, B. (2010, August 23). Inside the secret world of Trader Joe's. *Fortune.* Retrieved from http://money.cnn.com/2010/08/20/news/companies/inside_trader_joes_full_version.fortune/index.htm

Kreft, W. (1993). *Ladenplanung: Merchandising-Architektur Strategie für Verkaufsräume.* Leinfelden-Echterdingen, Germany: Verlagsanstalt Alexander Koch.

Kroeber-Riel, W. (1993). *Bildkommunikation: Imagerystrategien für die Werbung.* München, Germany: Vahlen.

Kroeber-Riel, W., Weinberg, P., & Groeppel-Klein, A. (2009). *Konsumentenverhalten* (9th ed.). München, Germany: Vahlen.

Kubota, Y. (2009). *Park plays high-pitch tone to discourage vandals.* Retrieved from http://www.reuters.com/assets/print?aid=USTRE54L4H620090525

Lash, E. (1998). Punchy point of purchase pointers. *Dairy Field Reports, 181*(9), 1.

Lehrner, J., Marwinski, G., Lehr, S., Johren, P., & Deecke, L. (2005). Ambient odors of orange and lavender reduce anxiety and improve mood in a dental office. *Physiology & Behavior, 86,* 92–95.

Leonard, T. (2008, July 14). The strange land where girls want to dress like their dolls. *The Daily Telegraph,* p. 22.

Levy, M., & Weitz, B. A. (2009). *Retailing management* (7th ed.). New York, NY: McGraw-Hill/Irwin.

Lewison, D. M. (1991). *Retailing* (4th ed.). New York, NY: Macmillan.

Lovelock, C. H., & Morgan, I. P. (1996). Euro Disney: An American in Paris. In C. H. Lovelock & J. Wirtz (Eds.), *Services marketing. People, technology, strategy* (3rd ed., pp. 127–140). Upper Saddle River, NJ: Pearson/Prentice Hall.

Lovelock, C. H., & Wirtz, J. (2011). *Services marketing: People, technology, strategy* (7th ed.). Boston, MA: Pearson.

Lynch, K. (1960). *The image of the city.* Cambridge, MA: MIT Press.

Machleit, K. A., Eroglu, S. A., & Mantel, S. P. (2000). Perceived retail crowding and shopping satisfaction: What modifies this relationship? *Journal of Consumer Psychology, 9*(1), 29–42.

MacInnis, D. J., & Park, C. W. (1991). The differential role of characteristics of music on high- and low-involvement consumers' processing of ads. *Journal of Consumer Research, 18*(2), 161–172.

Magee, E. (2010). What's at eye level in your refrigerator? Retrieved from http://blogs.webmd.com/healthy-recipe-doctor/2010/07/whats-at-eye-level-in-your-refrigerator.html

Maister, D. H. (1984). The psychology of waiting lines. *Harvard Business School Note 9-684-064, 49-684-064* (Rev. 5/8).

Mattila, A. S., & Wirtz, J. (2001). Congruency of scent and music as a driver of in-store evaluations and behavior. *Journal of Retailing, 77*(2), 273–289.

McGoun, E. G., Dunkak, W. H., Bettner, M. S., & Allen, D. E. (2003). Walt's street and Wall Street: Theming, theater, and experience in finance. *Critical Perspectives on Accounting, 14*(6), 647–661.

McKinnon, G. F., Kelly, P. J., & Robison, D. E. (1981). Sales effects of point-of-purchase in-store signing. *Journal of Retailing, 57*(2), 49–63.

Mehrabian, A., & Russell, J. A. (1974). *An approach to environmental psychology.* Cambridge, MA: MIT Press.

Meyer, W. G., Harris, E. E., Kohns, D. P., Stone, J. R., & Ashmun, R. D. (1988). *Retail Marketing* (8th ed.). New York, NY: McGraw-Hill Ryerson.

Miller, G. A. (1956). The magical number seven, plus or minus two: Some limits on our capacity for processing information. *Psychological Review, 101*(2), 343–352.

Milliman, R. E. (1982). Using background music to affect the behavior of supermarket shoppers. *Journal of Marketing, 46*(3), 88–91.

Milliman, R. E. (1986). The influence of background music on the behavior of restaurant patrons. *The Journal of Consumer Research, 13*(2), 286–289.

Mills, A. (n.d.) Parking signs rules: Is your parking lot compliant? Retrieved from http://ezinearticles.com/?Parking-Signs-Rules---Is-Your-Parking-Lot-Compliant?&id=2001413

Mitchell, D. J., Kahn, B. E., & Knasko, S. C. (1995). There's something in the air: Effects of congruent or incongruent ambient odor on consumer decision making. *The Journal of Consumer Research, 22*(2), 229–238.

Mitrasinovic, M. (1998). Theme parks. (Doctoral dissertation). University of Florida, Gainesville, FL.

Mongello, L. (2006). Mickey's 10 commandments by Marty Sklar. Retrieved from http://www.wdwradio.com/forums/walt-disney-company/5635-mickeys-10-commandments-marty-sklar.html

Moore, C. M., Doherty, A. M., & Doyle, S. A. (2010). Flagship stores as a market entry method: The perspective of luxury fashion retailing. *European Journal of Marketing, 44*(1/2), 139–161.

Morin, S. (1983, January 10). Interior design sets out to make casino that relaxes your morality. *The Wall Street Journal*, p. 31.

Nation. (1998). Nation's last themeless restaurant closes. Retrieved from http://www.theonion.com/articles/nations-last-themeless-restaurant-closes,3907

O'Connell, B. (2008, November 21). In a window wonderland. *The Irish Times*, p. 17.

Oldenburg, R. (1999). *The great good place: Cafés, coffee shops, bookstores, bars, hair salons, and other hangouts at the heart of a community*. New York, NY: Marlowe.

O'Neill, K. (2009, September 14). Mark's goes beyond "cool" look: Chain offers walk-in freezer so consumers can test clothes in Canadian winter conditions. *The Globe and Mail*, p. B5.

O'Shea, J. (2003, March 19). Empty shop fronts offer window on artwork. *UK Newsquest Regional Press*, p. 17.

Packaging research. (1983). Packaging research probes stopping power, label reading, and consumer attitudes among the targeted audience. *Marketing News, 17*(15), 8.

Packard, V. O. (1958). *The hidden persuaders*. New York, NY: Pocket Books.

Paivio, A. (1991). *Images in mind: The evolution of a theory*. New York, NY: Harvester Wheatsheaf.

Penn, M. J., & Zalesne, E. K. (2007). *Microtrends: The small forces behind tomorrow's big changes*. New York, NY: Twelve.

Pepper, A. (1993, January 4). Scents and cents: Experts advising more and more merchants to use smell to sell. *Orange County Register*, E01.

Pine, B. J., & Gilmore, J. H. (1999). *The experience economy: Work is theatre & every business a stage*. Boston, MA: Harvard Business School Press.

Rook, D. W., & Hoch, S. J. (1985). Consuming impulse. *Advances in Consumer Research, 12*, 23–27.

Russell, J. A., & Mehrabian, A. (1976). Environmental variables in consumer research. *Journal of Consumer Research, 3*(1), 62–63.

Sanders, A. F. (1963). *The selective process in the functional visual field*. Soesterberg, Netherlands: The Institute of Perception.

Sands, D. (1984). The next approach from Hepworths. *Retail and Distribution Management, 12*(6), 30–31.

Schmitt, B., & Simonson, A. (1997). *Marketing aesthetics: The strategic management of brands, identity, and image.* New York, NY: Free Press.

Sen, S., Block, L. G., & Chandran, S. (2002). Window displays and consumer shopping decisions. *Journal of Retailing and Consumer Services, 9*(5), 277–290.

Shakespeare, W. (2009). *As You Like It: The Cambridge Dover Wilson Shakespeare.* Cambridge, UK: Cambridge University Press

Smilansky, S. (2009). *Experiential marketing: A practical guide to interactive brand experiences.* London, UK: Kogan Page.

Smith, P., & Burns, D. J. (1996). Atmospherics and retail environments: The case of the "power aisle." *International Journal of Retail & Distribution Management, 24*(1), 7.

Solomon, M. R., Bamossy, G., Askegaard, S., & Hogg, M. K. (2006). *Consumer behaviour: A European perspective* (3rd ed.). Harlow, UK: Financial Times.

Sommer, R., & Aitkens, S. (1982). Mental mapping of two supermarkets. *Journal of Consumer Research, 9*(2), 211.

Sorensen, H. (2009). *Inside the mind of the shopper: The science of retailing.* Upper Saddle River, NJ: Pearson Prentice Hall.

Spangenberg, E., Crowley, A. E., & Henderson, P. W. (1996). Improving the store environment. Do olfactory cues affect evaluations and behaviors? *Journal of Marketing, 60*(2), 67–80.

Spector, A. (1999). Levy-Spielberg group scuttles Dive! Prototype locale. *Nation's Restaurant News, 33*(5), 6.

Spies, K., Hesse, F., & Loesch, K. (1997). Store atmosphere, mood and purchasing behavior. *International Journal of Research in Marketing, 14*(1), 1–17.

Storefronts. (1996). Storefronts show advantage of curb appeal. *Chain Store Age, 72*(11), 102.

Stratton, V. N., & Zalanowski, A. (1984). The effect of background music on verbal interaction in groups. *Journal of Music Therapy, 21*(1), 16–26.

Summers, T. (2001). Shedding some light on store atmospherics: Influence of illumination on consumer behavior. *Journal of Business Research, 54*(2), 145–150.

Sweeney, J. C., & Wyber, F. (2002). The role of cognitions and emotions in the music-approach-avoidance behavior relationship. *Journal of Services Marketing, 16*(1), 51–69.

Taylor, J. (2004, June 6). Business signs are paramount. *The Houston Chronicle,* p. 4.

Tips. (1995, September 6). Tips for business success. *Business Times* (Malaysia), p. 6.

Tolman, E. C. (1984). Cognitive maps in rats and men. *Psychological Review, 55*(4), 189–208.

Traindl, A. (2007). *Neuromarketing: Die innovative Visualisierung von Emotionen* (3rd ed.). Linz, Austria: Trauner.

Trilling, L. (1972). *Sincerity and authenticity.* London, UK: Oxford University Press.

Turley, T. W., & Milliman, R. E. (2000). Atmospheric effects on shopping behavior: A review of the experimental evidence. *Journal of Business Research, 49*(2), 193–211.

Underhill, P. (1999). *Why we buy: The science of shopping.* New York, NY: Simon & Schuster.

van der Waerden, P., Borgers, A., & Timmermans, H. (1998). The impact of the parking situation in shopping centres on store choice behaviour. *Geo Journal, 45*(4), 309–315.

Vence, D. L. (2007). Point of purchase displays. *Marketing News, 41*(18), 8.

Veryzer, R. W., & Hutchinson, W. J. (1998). The influence of unity and prototypicality on aesthetic response to new product design. *Journal of Consumer Research, 24*(4), 374–394.

Vincent, G. K., & Velkoff, V. A. (2010). *The next four decades, the older population in the United States: 2010 to 2050: Current population reports.* Washington, DC: U.S. Department of Commerce, Economics and Statistics Administration.

Wal-Mart. (2010). *Walmart annual report 2010.* Bentonville, AR: Author. Retrieved from http://investors.walmartstores.com/phoenix.zhtml?c=112761&p=irol-reportsannual

Wedel, M., & Pieters, R. (Eds.). (2008). *Visual marketing: From attention to action.* New York, NY: Taylor & Francis.

Weinberg, P. (1992). *Erlebnismarketing.* München, Germany: Vahlen.

Wertheimer, M. (1922). Untersuchungen zur Lehre von der Gestalt. *Psychologische Forschung, 1*(1), 47–58.

Wexner, L. B. (1954). The degree to which colors (hues) are associated with mood-tones. *Journal of Applied Psychology, 38*(6), 432–435.

Wilkie, M. (1995). Scent of a market. *American Demographics, 17*(8), 40.

Wilkie, W. L. (1994). *Consumer behavior* (3rd ed.). New York, NY: Wiley.

Yalch, R. F., & Spangenberg, E. R. (1988). An environmental psychological study of foreground and background music as retail atmospheric factors. In A. W. Walle (Ed.), *American Marketing Association educators' conference proceedings* (pp. 106–110). Chicago, IL: AMA.

Yalch, R. F., & Spangenberg, E. R. (1990). Effects of store music on shopping behavior. *The Journal of Consumer Marketing, 7*(2), 55–63.

Illustration Credits

Introduction

Figure I.1: Riem Khalil

Chapter 1

Figures 1.1–1.10: Riem Khalil

Figure 1.11: Reprinted with permission of Umdasch Shop-Concept

Figures 1.12–1.19: Riem Khalil

Chapter 2

Figures 2.1–2.13: Riem Khalil

Chapter 3

Figures 3.1, 3.2: Riem Khalil

Figure 3.3: Glow, "Mall Cairns," CC-Lizenz (BY 2.0), http://creativecommons.org/licenses/by/2.0/de/deed.de; *source*: http://www.piqs.de

Figure 3.4: schorse1963, "Einkaufszentrum," CC-Lizenz (BY 2.0), http://creativecommons.org/licenses/by/2.0/de/deed.de; *source*: http://www.piqs.de

Figures 3.5, 3.6: Riem Khalil

Figures 3.7, 3.8: Reprinted with permission of Umdasch Shop-Concept

Figures 3.9, 3.10: Riem Khalil

Chapter 4

Figure 4.1: Reprinted with permission of Umdasch Shop-Concept

Figure 4.2: Riem Khalil

Figure 4.3: Umdasch Shop-Concept

Figures 4.4–4.8: Riem Khalil

Figure 4.9: Peter Dutton, "Lego People," CC-Lizenz (BY 2.0), http://creativecommons.org/licenses/by/2.0/de/deed.de; *source*: http://www.piqs.de

Figure 4.10: Riem Khalil

Figure 4.11: Umdasch Shop-Concept

Figure 4.12: Riem Khalil

Figure 4.13: Umdasch Shop-Concept

Figures 4.14–4.17: Riem Khalil

Figures 4.18, 4.19: Umdasch Shop-Concept

Chapter 5

Figures 5.1–5.5: Riem Khalil

Figure 5.6: Umdasch Shop-Concept

Figures 5.7–5.9: Riem Khalil

Chapter 6

Figures 6.1–6.2: Riem Khalil

Figure 6.3: Reproduced with permission of American Girl Brands LLC

Figure 6.4: Riem Khalil

Figure 6.5: Reproduced with permission of Barnes & Noble, Inc.

Chapter 7

Figures 7.1, 7.2: Riem Khalil

Figure 7.3: Reprinted with permission of Meyer-Hentschel Institute

Figure 7.4: Riem Khalil

Figure 7.5: Reprinted with permission of Umdasch Shop-Concept

Index

The italicized *f* and *t* following page numbers refer to figures and tables, respectively.

Announcing the Business Expert Press Digital Library

Concise E-books Business Students Need for Classroom and Research

This book can also be purchased in an e-book collection by your library as

- a one-time purchase,
- that is owned forever,
- allows for simultaneous readers,
- has no restrictions on printing, and
- can be downloaded as PDFs from within the library community.

Our digital library collections are a great solution to beat the rising cost of textbooks. e-books can be loaded into their course management systems or onto student's e-book readers.

The **Business Expert Press** digital libraries are very affordable, with no obligation to buy in future years.

For more information, please visit **www.businessexpert.com/libraries**. To set up a trial in the United States, please contact **Sheri Allen** at *sheri.allen@globalepress.com*; for all other regions, contact **Nicole Lee** at *nicole.lee@igroupnet.com*.

CONSUMER BEHAVIOR
Collection Editor: **Naresh Malhotra**

Consumer Behavior: Women and Shopping by Patricia Huddleston and Stella Minahan.

0 1341 1488287 8

CPSIA information can be obtained at www.ICGtesting.com
Printed in the USA
BVOW010607020512

289181BV00005B/4/P

9 781606 490945

Mitrasinovic, M. (1998). Theme parks. (Doctoral dissertation). University of Florida, Gainesville, FL.

Mongello, L. (2006). Mickey's 10 commandments by Marty Sklar. Retrieved from http://www.wdwradio.com/forums/walt-disney-company/5635-mickeys-10-commandments-marty-sklar.html

Moore, C. M., Doherty, A. M., & Doyle, S. A. (2010). Flagship stores as a market entry method: The perspective of luxury fashion retailing. *European Journal of Marketing, 44*(1/2), 139–161.

Morin, S. (1983, January 10). Interior design sets out to make casino that relaxes your morality. *The Wall Street Journal*, p. 31.

Nation. (1998). Nation's last themeless restaurant closes. Retrieved from http://www.theonion.com/articles/nations-last-themeless-restaurant-closes,3907

O'Connell, B. (2008, November 21). In a window wonderland. *The Irish Times*, p. 17.

Oldenburg, R. (1999). *The great good place: Cafés, coffee shops, bookstores, bars, hair salons, and other hangouts at the heart of a community*. New York, NY: Marlowe.

O'Neill, K. (2009, September 14). Mark's goes beyond "cool" look: Chain offers walk-in freezer so consumers can test clothes in Canadian winter conditions. *The Globe and Mail*, p. B5.

O'Shea, J. (2003, March 19). Empty shop fronts offer window on artwork. *UK Newsquest Regional Press*, p. 17.

Packaging research. (1983). Packaging research probes stopping power, label reading, and consumer attitudes among the targeted audience. *Marketing News, 17*(15), 8.

Packard, V. O. (1958). *The hidden persuaders*. New York, NY: Pocket Books.

Paivio, A. (1991). *Images in mind: The evolution of a theory*. New York, NY: Harvester Wheatsheaf.

Penn, M. J., & Zalesne, E. K. (2007). *Microtrends: The small forces behind tomorrow's big changes*. New York, NY: Twelve.

Pepper, A. (1993, January 4). Scents and cents: Experts advising more and more merchants to use smell to sell. *Orange County Register*, E01.

Pine, B. J., & Gilmore, J. H. (1999). *The experience economy: Work is theatre & every business a stage*. Boston, MA: Harvard Business School Press.

Rook, D. W., & Hoch, S. J. (1985). Consuming impulse. *Advances in Consumer Research, 12*, 23–27.

Russell, J. A., & Mehrabian, A. (1976). Environmental variables in consumer research. *Journal of Consumer Research, 3*(1), 62–63.

Sanders, A. F. (1963). *The selective process in the functional visual field*. Soesterberg, Netherlands: The Institute of Perception.

Sands, D. (1984). The next approach from Hepworths. *Retail and Distribution Management, 12*(6), 30–31.

Schmitt, B., & Simonson, A. (1997). *Marketing aesthetics: The strategic management of brands, identity, and image.* New York, NY: Free Press.

Sen, S., Block, L. G., & Chandran, S. (2002). Window displays and consumer shopping decisions. *Journal of Retailing and Consumer Services, 9*(5), 277–290.

Shakespeare, W. (2009). *As You Like It: The Cambridge Dover Wilson Shakespeare.* Cambridge, UK: Cambridge University Press

Smilansky, S. (2009). *Experiential marketing: A practical guide to interactive brand experiences.* London, UK: Kogan Page.

Smith, P., & Burns, D. J. (1996). Atmospherics and retail environments: The case of the "power aisle." *International Journal of Retail & Distribution Management, 24*(1), 7.

Solomon, M. R., Bamossy, G., Askegaard, S., & Hogg, M. K. (2006). *Consumer behaviour: A European perspective* (3rd ed.). Harlow, UK: Financial Times.

Sommer, R., & Aitkens, S. (1982). Mental mapping of two supermarkets. *Journal of Consumer Research, 9*(2), 211.

Sorensen, H. (2009). *Inside the mind of the shopper: The science of retailing.* Upper Saddle River, NJ: Pearson Prentice Hall.

Spangenberg, E., Crowley, A. E., & Henderson, P. W. (1996). Improving the store environment. Do olfactory cues affect evaluations and behaviors? *Journal of Marketing, 60*(2), 67–80.

Spector, A. (1999). Levy-Spielberg group scuttles Dive! Prototype locale. *Nation's Restaurant News, 33*(5), 6.

Spies, K., Hesse, F., & Loesch, K. (1997). Store atmosphere, mood and purchasing behavior. *International Journal of Research in Marketing, 14*(1), 1–17.

Storefronts. (1996). Storefronts show advantage of curb appeal. *Chain Store Age, 72*(11), 102.

Stratton, V. N., & Zalanowski, A. (1984). The effect of background music on verbal interaction in groups. *Journal of Music Therapy, 21*(1), 16–26.

Summers, T. (2001). Shedding some light on store atmospherics: Influence of illumination on consumer behavior. *Journal of Business Research, 54*(2), 145–150.

Sweeney, J. C., & Wyber, F. (2002). The role of cognitions and emotions in the music-approach-avoidance behavior relationship. *Journal of Services Marketing, 16*(1), 51–69.

Taylor, J. (2004, June 6). Business signs are paramount. *The Houston Chronicle,* p. 4.

Tips. (1995, September 6). Tips for business success. *Business Times* (Malaysia), p. 6.

Tolman, E. C. (1984). Cognitive maps in rats and men. *Psychological Review, 55*(4), 189–208.

Traindl, A. (2007). *Neuromarketing: Die innovative Visualisierung von Emotionen* (3rd ed.). Linz, Austria: Trauner.

Trilling, L. (1972). *Sincerity and authenticity.* London, UK: Oxford University Press.

Turley, T. W., & Milliman, R. E. (2000). Atmospheric effects on shopping behavior: A review of the experimental evidence. *Journal of Business Research, 49*(2), 193–211.

Underhill, P. (1999). *Why we buy: The science of shopping.* New York, NY: Simon & Schuster.

van der Waerden, P., Borgers, A., & Timmermans, H. (1998). The impact of the parking situation in shopping centres on store choice behaviour. *Geo Journal, 45*(4), 309–315.

Vence, D. L. (2007). Point of purchase displays. *Marketing News, 41*(18), 8.

Veryzer, R. W., & Hutchinson, W. J. (1998). The influence of unity and proto-typicality on aesthetic response to new product design. *Journal of Consumer Research, 24*(4), 374–394.

Vincent, G. K., & Velkoff, V. A. (2010). *The next four decades, the older population in the United States: 2010 to 2050: Current population reports.* Washington, DC: U.S. Department of Commerce, Economics and Statistics Administration.

Wal-Mart. (2010). *Walmart annual report 2010.* Bentonville, AR: Author. Retrieved from http://investors.walmartstores.com/phoenix.zhtml?c=112761&p=irol-reportsannual

Wedel, M., & Pieters, R. (Eds.). (2008). *Visual marketing: From attention to action.* New York, NY: Taylor & Francis.

Weinberg, P. (1992). *Erlebnismarketing.* München, Germany: Vahlen.

Wertheimer, M. (1922). Untersuchungen zur Lehre von der Gestalt. *Psychologische Forschung, 1*(1), 47–58.

Wexner, L. B. (1954). The degree to which colors (hues) are associated with mood-tones. *Journal of Applied Psychology, 38*(6), 432–435.

Wilkie, M. (1995). Scent of a market. *American Demographics, 17*(8), 40.

Wilkie, W. L. (1994). *Consumer behavior* (3rd ed.). New York, NY: Wiley.

Yalch, R. F., & Spangenberg, E. R. (1988). An environmental psychological study of foreground and background music as retail atmospheric factors. In A. W. Walle (Ed.), *American Marketing Association educators' conference proceedings* (pp. 106–110). Chicago, IL: AMA.

Yalch, R. F., & Spangenberg, E. R. (1990). Effects of store music on shopping behavior. *The Journal of Consumer Marketing, 7*(2), 55–63.

Illustration Credits

Introduction

Figure I.1: Riem Khalil

Chapter 1

Figures 1.1–1.10: Riem Khalil

Figure 1.11: Reprinted with permission of Umdasch Shop-Concept

Figures 1.12–1.19: Riem Khalil

Chapter 2

Figures 2.1–2.13: Riem Khalil

Chapter 3

Figures 3.1, 3.2: Riem Khalil

Figure 3.3: Glow, "Mall Cairns," CC-Lizenz (BY 2.0), http://creativecommons.org/licenses/by/2.0/de/deed.de; *source*: http://www.piqs.de

Figure 3.4: schorse1963, "Einkaufszentrum," CC-Lizenz (BY 2.0), http://creativecommons.org/licenses/by/2.0/de/deed.de; *source*: http://www.piqs.de

Figures 3.5, 3.6: Riem Khalil

Figures 3.7, 3.8: Reprinted with permission of Umdasch Shop-Concept

Figures 3.9, 3.10: Riem Khalil

Chapter 4

Figure 4.1: Reprinted with permission of Umdasch Shop-Concept

Figure 4.2: Riem Khalil

Figure 4.3: Umdasch Shop-Concept

Figures 4.4–4.8: Riem Khalil

Figure 4.9: Peter Dutton, "Lego People," CC-Lizenz (BY 2.0), http://creativecommons.org/licenses/by/2.0/de/deed.de; *source*: http://www.piqs.de

Figure 4.10: Riem Khalil

Figure 4.11: Umdasch Shop-Concept

Figure 4.12: Riem Khalil

Figure 4.13: Umdasch Shop-Concept

Figures 4.14–4.17: Riem Khalil

Figures 4.18, 4.19: Umdasch Shop-Concept

Chapter 5

Figures 5.1–5.5: Riem Khalil

Figure 5.6: Umdasch Shop-Concept

Figures 5.7–5.9: Riem Khalil

Chapter 6

Figures 6.1–6.2: Riem Khalil

Figure 6.3: Reproduced with permission of American Girl Brands LLC

Figure 6.4: Riem Khalil

Figure 6.5: Reproduced with permission of Barnes & Noble, Inc.

Chapter 7

Figures 7.1, 7.2: Riem Khalil

Figure 7.3: Reprinted with permission of Meyer-Hentschel Institute

Figure 7.4: Riem Khalil

Figure 7.5: Reprinted with permission of Umdasch Shop-Concept

Index

The italicized *f* and *t* following page numbers refer to figures and tables, respectively.

Announcing the Business Expert Press Digital Library

Concise E-books Business Students Need for Classroom and Research

This book can also be purchased in an e-book collection by your library as

- a one-time purchase,
- that is owned forever,
- allows for simultaneous readers,
- has no restrictions on printing, and
- can be downloaded as PDFs from within the library community.

Our digital library collections are a great solution to beat the rising cost of textbooks. e-books can be loaded into their course management systems or onto student's e-book readers.

The **Business Expert Press** digital libraries are very affordable, with no obligation to buy in future years.

For more information, please visit **www.businessexpert.com/libraries**. To set up a trial in the United States, please contact **Sheri Allen** at *sheri.allen@globalepress.com*; for all other regions, contact **Nicole Lee** at *nicole.lee@igroupnet.com*.

CONSUMER BEHAVIOR
Collection Editor: **Naresh Malhotra**

Consumer Behavior: Women and Shopping by Patricia Huddleston and Stella Minahan.

CPSIA information can be obtained at www.ICGtesting.com
Printed in the USA
BVOW010607020512

289181BV00005B/4/P